391

Housing Conditions

IN

Manchester and Salford

Uniform with this volume.

A SUPPLEMENTARY VOLUME, ENTITLED

The Improvement of the Dwellings and Surroundings of the People

THE EXAMPLE OF GERMANY

By T. C. HORSFALL,

President of the Citizens' Association,

IS PUBLISHED WITH THIS REPORT.

Price, in Paper Cover, One Shilling net ;
In Cloth, Two Shillings net.

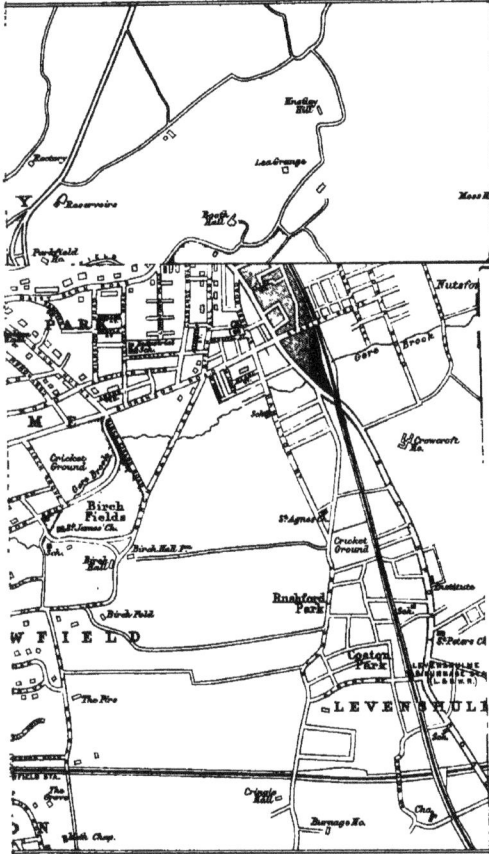

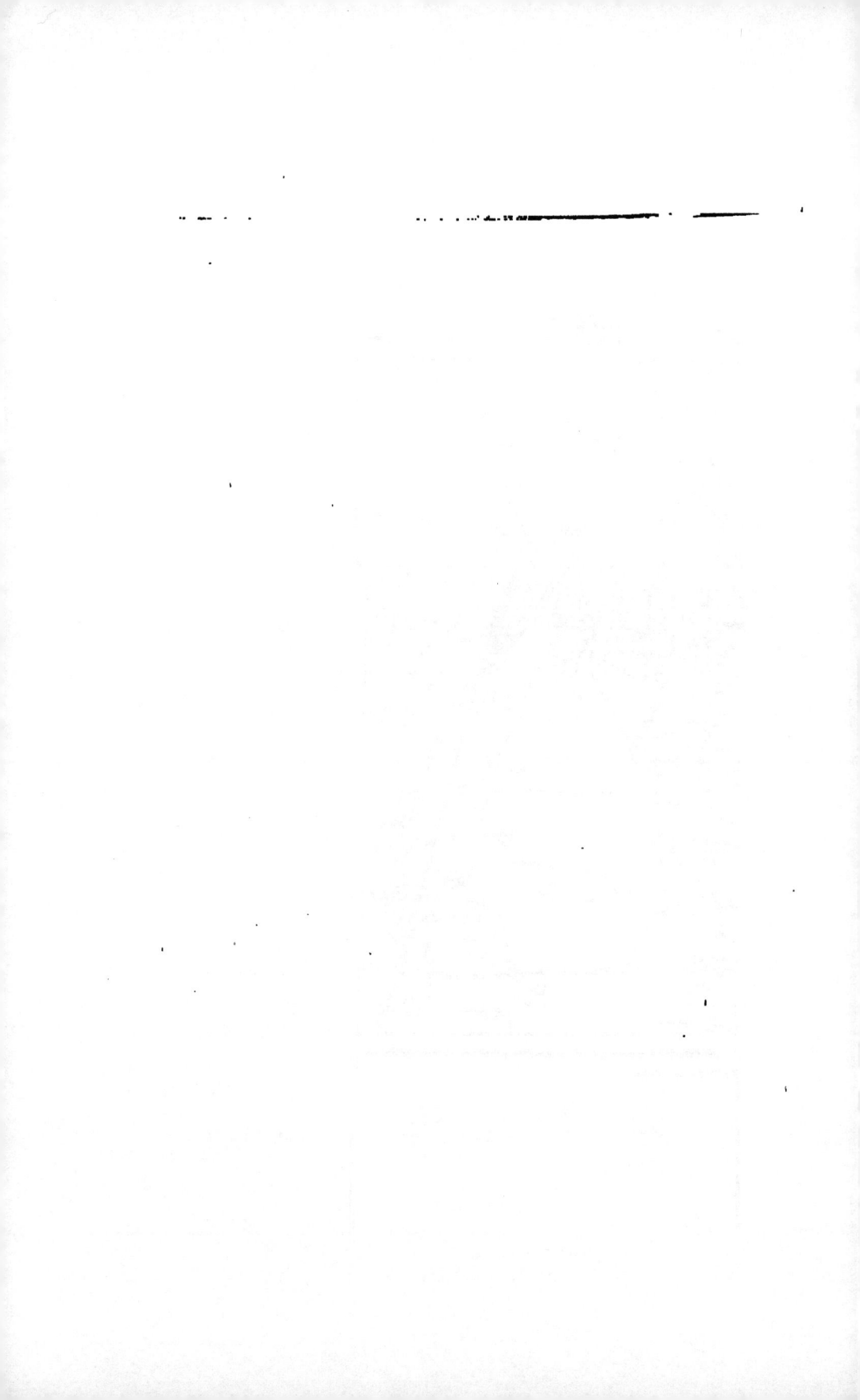

Housing Conditions

IN

MANCHESTER & SALFORD

*A Report prepared for the Citizens' Association for
the Improvement of the Unwholesome Dwellings
and Surroundings of the People, with the aid of
the Executive Committee*

BY

T. R. MARR

Secretary of the Citizens' Association

SHERRATT AND HUGHES
MANCHESTER AND LONDON

—

1904

PREFACE.

We ask those who read the following pages to consider carefully what is there set forth. We have studiously avoided exaggeration in our descriptions of existing evils, and we have stated, with a quietness befitting the depth of our convictions, the reforms which we consider to be needful. We hope that many men and women will be touched by the appeal which we make for those who live under less favourable conditions than themselves. To such persons the Citizens' Association offers the opportunity of trying to remove the evils indicated in this Report. Help, given in the form of money, of personal service, or simply in encouragement, will be welcomed. The Association is only at the beginning of its work. Having shown that grave evils exist, it intends to work till those evils have been removed or greatly mitigated. Doubtless as time passes fresh fields of enquiry and of action will open to it, and fresh suggestions as to ways of making life in Manchester and Salford healthier and happier will be made and considered. If success is to be attained, the membership of the Association must be greatly increased.

Readers of the Report must remember that, although many districts in a great city have a well marked general character, in each such district there are houses which are of an exceptional kind. The map which we give as a frontispiece does not attempt to do more than indicate the general character of areas. Every house in an area of one colour does not answer to the description given to that colour; it is enough that most of the houses answer to the description. It must be noted that the colour assigned to "Warehouses, Offices," etc., is also used for Public Buildings such as the Assize Courts and Workhouses.

Much kind assistance has been given us while we have been preparing this volume, to the givers of which we desire to express our cordial thanks. We wish especially to acknowledge the help given us by Mr. J. R. Corbett, M.A., Surveyor, in preparing the map and in providing us with illustrations.

TABLE OF CONTENTS.

" Of all the great social problems of modern times incident to the growth of cities, none is claiming public attention in a greater degree than that of the housing of the working people. Mere *housing*, however, that is, merely shelter, does not solve this problem. It only aggravates it by herding men and women together under conditions which inevitably tend to produce disease and crime. It is only by providing *homes* for the working people, that is, by providing for them not only shelter, *but shelter of such kind as to protect life and health and to make family life possible, free from surroundings which tend to immorality*, that the evils of crowded city life can be mitigated and overcome. Nor does it concern only the working classes who are to be sheltered. It is of vital moment to all the inhabitants of every city, and particularly to those of every city governed by democratic rule. Homes are quite as much needed to make good citizens as to make good men. According as the working people are provided with better or poorer homes will the government, morals and health of a city be better or worse."— *Report of the Tenement House Commission, New York.*

" Moreover, modern civilization not merely draws the mass of workers from a fixed habitation upon the soil, with those attachments of place which have helped so much to build the character of great nations; it has not planted them firmly in city life. Vast numbers are fated to a life of wandering over the face of a great city, driven hither and thither by the shifting tide of employments and substituting for the constant *Home* a narrow temporary *Shelter*. The material structure of sound family life is thus grievously impaired; the economic power of landlordism, in narrowing the shelter of the workers, plays into the hands of the publican, whose premises form a natural, almost a necessary, annex of the worker's home for the husband and father, as the slum-street is for the children."—*The Social Problem*, by John A. Hobson.

Housing Conditions in Manchester and Salford.

CHAPTER I.

CERTAIN facts as to the unwholesome and degrading surroundings amid which some of our fellow citizens live are recorded in the following pages. We believe that many people in Manchester and Salford must be ignorant of the facts, since such conditions are allowed to exist. The reports prepared yearly by the Medical Officers of Health tell the same story, but unfortunately few people read those reports and still fewer realise their significance.

Year by year it is shown in the reports that in some districts the death-rate, especially for young children, is much above the average for the whole town. This is sure evidence that the conditions of life in these districts are unsatisfactory. There are two factors in the production of a high death-rate to which we would draw especial attention, *poverty*, and *unwholesome houses and surroundings*. Other things doubtless contribute to make life in these districts poorer in length of days and in achievement than in more favoured places. Chief among these other factors stand drunkenness, thriftlessness and betting, all due to lack of character and purpose in life.

It has not lain within the scope of our present work to try to ascertain the amount of poverty in the towns. The recent enquiries of Mr. Rowntree and of Mr. Booth have given results which we believe can safely be applied to Manchester and Salford (p. 24). We estimate that upwards of 212,000 persons are in a state of poverty, and of these more than 75,000 are in a state of severe poverty (Mr. Rowntree's " primary " poverty).

Our immediate task has been to collect materials which would enable us to describe the houses and surroundings of the people where the conditions are not good. A systematic survey has been made of a few areas, chosen because we had reason to

b

believe the conditions there were bad, though not the worst that
could be found.   In these areas, described in Chap. IV., we
found many families living under conditions which make decent
life well-nigh impossible.   We have endeavoured to avoid
highly-coloured pictures of life in the slums, and to put before
the citizens of Manchester and Salford the bare facts.   We may
here summarise these facts : —

(a) Many houses, at present occupied, are unwholesome
because they have been badly built or are in need of repair.
Such houses are frequently damp and cold.   Many of them are
old and dirty.

(b) Many back-to-back houses (which most sanitary authorities say are unwholesome) still exist and are occupied.

(c) Scores of houses are without a separate water supply.
This certainly tends to discourage cleanliness, and to lower the
standard of health.

(d) In scores of cases a house has a closet shared by from
two to eight houses.   In many instances the closets are badly
kept, and they are often so placed as to offend all sense of
decency.

(e) The rooms of many houses are too dark for healthy life.
This in some places results from overshadowing by high
buildings and walls; but more frequently from the narrowness
of the street.

(f) From similar causes many houses do not get sufficient
air.

(g) Many houses have too many people living in them for
the size and number of the rooms.

(h) Whole districts have more houses to the acre than is
consistent with health, and no district has enough open spaces
and playgrounds.

(i) The rents paid for the houses where the conditions are
unwholesome are, on the average, very little lower than those
paid for good houses in other parts of the town.

Faced with these facts, we have to urge : —

(1) That a *comprehensive housing policy be formed for the
whole Manchester-Salford area*, including the suburban and

intermediate districts as well as those in the centre. Until such a policy is adopted we cannot hope for a solution of our difficulties. At present, while houses in the poorer districts are being closed, new residential districts are arising which, for lack of a real policy, will before many years be little better than slums. A comprehensive policy, as we understand it, would provide not only for the demolition of unwholesome dwellings and the statutory obligation to re-house the occupants, but would also definitely provide for the growth of the towns, planning roads, streets and open spaces for the new districts long before they are actually required for building.

The authorities of many German towns have plans prepared showing how new districts must be laid out, and in this way are able to ensure that the surroundings of the dwellings shall be wholesome. (See p. 89).† We might well imitate this procedure. New building bye-laws are needed, and the provision of these also forms part of a real housing policy.

(2) That the admirable work of the Sanitary Departments needs extension. More inspectors are required. Dr. Niven has suggested the need for a house-to-house investigation of one of the Sanitary Districts of Manchester. We are convinced that the authorities ought to undertake such an investigation continuously for the whole of Manchester and Salford, for the prevention of bad conditions rather than their cure when they have arisen. In all towns, small as well as large, experience has proved that only by a system of careful supervision continuously exercised by competent inspectors, is it possible to maintain the conditions essential for health.

(3) That the Town Councils should use more fully the powers they possess under the Housing of the Working Classes Acts of 1890 and 1900,* and erect in many different parts of the towns and of the country contiguous to the towns, groups of working-class dwellings, exemplary in respect of size and arrangement of rooms and of offices, and of pleasantness of exterior, and provided with adequate yard space and with small gardens. The objects of this work, which should be self-

---

† See, also, Supplementary Volume : " The Example of Germany."
* See, also, the Housing of the Working Classes Act, 1903.

supporting, should be (a) to provide part of the supply of wholesome dwellings needed by the towns, (b) to raise the working-man's ideal of a dwelling, and (c) to set a higher standard for those who are building or may build workmen's dwellings.

(4) That, as the task of supplying the whole number of potentially wholesome houses needed by the two towns is far beyond their power, the Town Councils should in all possible ways stimulate and help the community to fulfil that large part of the task which they cannot undertake, seeking if necessary fresh powers from Parliament to enable them to give the requisite stimulus and help. In addition to professional builders, who will probably always be the chief suppliers of houses, well-to-do persons desirous of promoting the public welfare and building societies may be expected, under favourable conditions, to provide a large number of dwellings.

As no house, however roomy, well-arranged and well-built, can be a wholesome dwelling if it have not wholesome surroundings, and as no private person can ensure that houses built by him shall have near them the wide streets, the open spaces, the vegetation, which are essential parts of wholesome environment, well-to-do citizens at present may well be prevented from building workmen's dwellings by the fear that any houses erected by them would be rendered unwholesome by the failure of the Town Councils to provide them with wholesome environment. For the purpose of ensuring that all buildings shall have wholesome environment, and of thus offering inducements to well-to-do philanthropic persons to take part in the task of providing houses for the working classes, it is necessary that Town Councils shall possess and use the power of making for all land still unbuilt on, in and near the towns, plans which must be strictly complied with by all who build on the land. These plans should indicate the position of all new streets, and should provide that the principal streets shall be wide and tree-planted, and that there shall be an ample amount of playground and other kinds of open space within easy reach of every group of houses.

If co-operative building societies, bound to provide their

members with wholesome houses at rents bearing a fixed relation to the cost of the houses, could easily be formed, probably many working people desirous of living in wholesome houses and of feeling assured that their rents would not be raised, would become members of them. The chief obstacle to the formation of such societies is the difficulty of obtaining capital at low rates of interest. It is desirable that here, as in some other countries, Town Councils shall have the power to obtain for building societies, whose objects and rules have their approval, and at low rates of interest, advances from public funds, savings-banks and insurance companies, sufficient to defray almost the whole cost of building.

(5)* That, as the land question lies at the root of the housing difficulty, the Town Councils should acquire as much land as possible, and that all land once obtained by a town should, as a rule, be held in perpetuity, sites for houses and other buildings being let for terms of years, and not sold, thus ensuring that the towns shall benefit by the unearned increment of value.

(6)* That Town Councils should have the power, which is possessed and used by many German towns, to levy a rate on unoccupied land within their areas, and that the declared value for rating purposes to be the purchase price if the town requires to buy the land. The exercise of this rating power has two good effects—it prevents, or tends to prevent, the owners of land in or near towns from leaving it unbuilt on until the " unearned incre- ment " of value reaches a very large amount and thus, by bringing land into the market earlier than it would otherwise be brought, it tends to keep down the price of land. Similarly it prevents the owners of unwholesome dwellings from allowing them to stand empty and forces them to either repair, replace, or sell the dwellings. It also provides a considerable sum annually which

---

* Professor Chapman, a member of the Committee, is unable to subscribe to the recommendation that unoccupied land should be rated, on the ground that he is not certain (a) as to the practicability of a suitable scheme, and (b) as to the effects and whether they would be desirable; and without considering further evidence and investigating the matter more fully, he is not prepared to endorse Recommendation 5 or its contrary.

can be used for the reduction of other rates. It is found that
the adoption of this system of rating, by establishing a trust-
worthy criterion of value, greatly reduces the number of appeals
against assessments for rates.

(7) That both our Town Councils and private builders in the
district should strive to attain in their building schemes—in the
general laying out of the sites as well as in the construction of
the houses—the admirable conditions obtaining in Bournville,
Port Sunlight, and other places which we have briefly described
(Chap. VI.). We have also described briefly the plan of adapt-
ing old property which is still in good condition to the needs
of the working classes. In Manchester work of this kind might
be done with much of the property in Chorlton-on-Medlock and
the neighbouring districts.

Our main purpose in including descriptions of housing
schemes adopted in other places has been to stimulate the
development of a comprehensive scheme for the improvement
of dwellings and their environment which all citizens may be
glad to help in carrying out.

(8) That our Town Councils should seek powers to enable
them to appoint Commissions, including not only members
of the Councils but other interested citizens, to consider the
needs of the locality and to make recommendations to the
Councils. A useful precedent has been afforded by the appoint-
ment of a Housing Commission in Glasgow, which has received
evidence on all sides of the question.

(9) That, in view of the difficulties which beset our Town
Councils, it is very desirable that the powers of such bodies
should be greatly extended, especially with regard to buying
land. We recognise, however, that it is useless to seek further
powers until fuller use is made of the powers which the Councils
already possess, and that it is, therefore, of the utmost importance to see that the persons sent to the Councils are prepared
to make use of these powers. We believe that the growing com-
plexity of modern municipal work makes it essential to have on
the local administrative bodies a larger proportion of experts
in the various departments, some of whom should be elected for
periods of many years, should give their whole time to the work

of the municipality and be adequately paid to do so. The system by which German towns obtain in their Town Councils a very effective combination of paid experts elected for long periods and of unpaid citizens elected for shorter periods of time is described in the Supplementary Volume. It deserves notice that of 23 persons who answered the question "Ought Mayors and the Chairmen of Committees of Town Councils to be appointed for long periods of time, and be paid salaries to enable them to give all their working time to the services of the community?" which was asked by the Association recently, 18 answered affirmatively, 1 ambiguously, and only 4 negatively.

What can be done at once is to see that the best possible men are sent to the Council Chambers to transact the work of the community. This rests ultimately, of course, with the citizens at large, and therefore in considerable degree with ministers of religion and others who can influence the opinions of their fellow citizens. Every possible effort should be made to dissociate elections to municipal office from political party organisation, and to put the interests of the whole community in the first place. We urge on every citizen that it is his duty to be conversant with the doings of the Town Councils and to weigh with the greatest care the qualifications of those who seek to represent him on those bodies.

To sum up. We see in our towns to-day many evils. Poor physique, impaired health, and premature senility; drunkenness, sexual immorality and other vice; betting and thriftlessness; decay of family life and lack of civic spirit; these are all too common. We find, too, poverty, houses unwholesome from many causes, lack of provision of open spaces and other means for healthy recreation, narrow and gloomy streets, an excessive amount of coal smoke, and a superabundance of public-houses. Endless discussion takes place among those interested in social reform as to which group of evils is cause, which effect. The truth seems to be that we have a vicious circle and that they are all both cause and effect. It is therefore necessary that all who are engaged in social work, all who are members of religious organisations, should join forces and at any sacrifice promote all measures for the welfare of the community.

CHAPTER II.

GENERAL ACCOUNT OF CONDITIONS IN MANCHESTER AND SALFORD.

Manchester and Salford are built upon a flat or slightly undulating stretch of ground, drained by the River Irwell. The Irwell receives within the city boundaries the waters of two tributary streams, the Medlock and the Irk.

The rivers in early times probably were of considerable value to the manufacturing interests of the towns, but now they are so polluted that they are a source of anxiety to those charged with the care of the public health.

The heights which are within easy reach of Manchester on all sides, save the west and south-west, are composed of lower coal measure or millstone-grit rocks. These high tablelands catch the moisture-laden clouds from the Atlantic, which are there condensed. Between the towns and the high lands comes the rich coalfield of South Lancashire, to which in large measure the prosperity of Manchester is due.

The area on which Manchester and Salford are actually built is covered by thick deposits of drift (boulder clay, sands and gravel), due to glacial action in a remote period. The clay has been worked to a large extent to provide the bricks with which the town has been built, and brickfields are still worked in the north of Manchester. In the northern district, where the ground gets higher, there is some sandstone quarrying.

The atmosphere of Manchester and Salford is exceedingly moist, owing to its situation in the track of the wet south-west winds.

HISTORY AND INDUSTRIES.

The growth of Manchester and Salford has been exceedingly rapid in the last century. Although the towns are of great age, they were relatively unimportant till the end of the eighteenth century, when the revolution in the methods of manufacturing textiles, especially cotton goods, caused the concentration of the great urban population now resident in the district.

During the nineteenth century the towns have spread rapidly over a considerable area, absorbing the smaller villages and townships which formerly lay just outside their boundaries. The rapid growth of the cotton industry and of other industries, such as engineering and chemical manufactures at first subsidiary to the cotton, and the concentration of the cotton "trade" in Manchester, have led to the sweeping away of many traces of the picturesque mediæval town which centred round the Cathedral. But bits of the old town are still to be seen, and in passing from the centre to the suburbs one may read in the buildings the history of the town. It is important to notice this history, as only in this way can we understand the origin of many of our present difficulties.

This history may be read in the buildings passed in journeying in almost any direction from the Cathedral to the outskirts of the town. We shall describe one such line. Starting from the old Jacobean houses near the Cathedral, belonging to a time when town and country were not so remote from each other as they are to-day, and passing through Angel Meadow to Rochdale Road, we may see some few eighteenth century houses. These may be known by their pillared porticoes. To-day they are in most cases given over to offices and workshops, though occasionally used as lodging-houses. Beyond we come to a district which marks the first period of expansion early in the nineteenth century, when houses, small and unwholesome and ill-supplied with sanitary requirements, were built near the factories and mills. There are our slums of the present time. Occasionally we find amongst such houses good older buildings which tell of a suburban or country house whose garden has been built over.

Still moving towards the outskirts of the town we pass through streets where the houses are mean, and seem on the down grade in many cases, but are supplied with sanitary conveniences and small yards. This records the beginning of modern municipal life when some care was taken to ensure that the houses reached a certain standard, though to our ideas a low one. Lastly, we reach the suburban area, where the houses are built according to modern bye-laws. They are better built and are well supplied with sanitary appliances, but the streets are monotonous to a degree. Houses of this description are, of course, not confined to the suburbs, but occur among the more recent houses in all parts of the town. In the suburban district proper we find houses which have gardens. This marks the districts to which the relatively well-to-do members of the community escape.

The accompanying plan of Manchester and Salford which we have prepared shows clearly the distribution of the industrial and residential areas. It will be seen that an irregular octopus-like figure covers the towns with arms reaching beyond the suburbs. The body part covers the central district surrounding Manchester Town Hall, which is given over almost entirely to shops, offices, warehouses, etc., and has a very small resident population. The arms represent the lines of communication and of transport which join the Manchester district to other places, i.e., the railway lines and the canals. It will be seen that alongside these the industries and workshops are gathered and that the residential districts lie between the arms. Near the centre where the space between the arms is least, the residential population is most crowded, and only towards the outside of the town do we find frequent open spaces.

The industries of the towns may be roughly grouped in two classes (a) the staple industries (as the manufactures of cotton, machinery, chemicals, etc., and (b) the minor industries. The differentiating factor in the two groups is the destination of the products. In the group of staple industries, the production is mainly for consumption outside the area, while in the minor industries the produce is mainly consumed within the area. The minor industries are those which have as their purpose to supply the immediate needs of the inhabitants of the towns, and chief among them stand the building and clothing trades, and the production and distribution of food and other articles required by the population. On the progress of the staple industries which find employment for many persons will chiefly depend the inflow of population to the district and its retention in the district; so that it may be said the staple industries determine the population. The minor industries, on the other hand, always grow in proportion to the population, since people must be housed, clothed and fed and get about their business. An immense number of people are therefore engaged in the building and furnishing trades, in the manufacture of clothing (part of which at least is intended for export), in baking and brewing, in shopkeeping and in the business of transport both of people and goods.

The industries of the district may be considered from three points of view—(a) their permanence, (b) their relation to health, and (c) the remuneration they offer to the workers engaged in them. The latter question is too large and difficult for us to express views on without much more evidence than we have obtained. While pursuing our investigations we have constantly tried to ascertain the wage of the chief worker in a household and the income of the family. We are aware that for statistical purposes information obtained in this way and which, in the majority of cases, we are not in a position to check is useless. Yet from our general knowledge of Manchester life we are persuaded that in very many cases the income of a family, even when work is steady and when the wages are carefully expended, is insufficient to maintain physical efficiency. The matter is discussed in the next section of this chapter.

Unskilled labourers in Manchester and Salford certainly earn low wages, under 20s. a week on the average, and they often have broken time when the income of the family sinks to nothing. On the other hand, the variety of industries in the towns and the large amount of almost unskilled labour required gives many opportunities for the younger members of families to find employment. The industries of Manchester and Salford also give employment to a very large number of women workers, among whom organisation is weak and wages are consequently low. In the poorer parts of the towns much harm results from the women going out to work. Not only do they themselves often suffer from exhaustion, but their families lack the care which is necessary if they are to grow up as good citizens. The children grow up of poor physique, often with feeble mental and moral powers, and fall into the ranks of the unskilled and unprofitable, who never can hope to earn decent wages, and are driven to live in the poorer kinds of houses. The housing question cannot be separated from the rest of the social problem.

According to our Medical Officer of Health, we in this district cannot say that our industries are unhealthy ones. It is true that in some cases they are carried on under unhealthy conditions, but these in most cases can be (and, thanks to vigilant inspection, are being) remedied. Although the industries in themselves may not be unhealthy the pressure at which people work in many cases leads to premature old age and breakdown.

The permanence of the industries in our district is, however, a point of prime importance in this discussion. If our industries or any considerable section of them are likely to move out of the district, it is certain that the population will move too. The pressure on house accommodation which we are about to consider in detail would then slacken, and reformers therefore need to weigh carefully any proposals for the further provision of houses. It has been remarked that cotton spinning and weaving are now mainly carried on outside Manchester and Salford; they have, in fact, been moved to the fringe of small towns encircling the greater ones. Will other industries follow suit? It is certainly possible, and many manufacturers seem tempted by the low price of land outside the towns. But even if the manufactures do go out, it seems probable that the work of distribution of goods will increasingly centre in this district, and will occupy more and more people, and there seems to us no reason for believing that the population of our towns is likely to decrease in the near future. Besides the manufactures are not likely to go far, and it will be seen that we contemplate the possibility of our towns controlling the distribution and housing of the population over much wider areas than they at present control.

POPULATION AND HEALTH.

In Manchester and Salford combined there is now a population of considerably over three-quarters of a million, and though the rate of increase has to some extent diminished, yet the figures given in the subjoined table show considerable actual increase.

POPULATION OF MANCHESTER AND SALFORD FROM 1841.

	City of Manchester.	Borough of Salford.	Totals.
Census of 1841	242,983*	70,224	313,207
,, 1851	303,382*	87,523	390,905
,, 1861	338,722*	102,449	441,171
,, 1871	351,189*	124,801	475,990
,, 1881	341,414*	176,235	517,649
,, 1881	373,583†	—	...... —
,, 1881	462,303‡	—	...... —
,, 1891	505,368‡	198,139	703,507
,, 1901	543,872‡	220,957	764,829

*Old area (4,293 acres). †Area as extended in 1885 (5,933 acres). ‡Area as extended in 1890 (12,935 acres).

It is obvious that without the expenditure of considerably more money and time than has been at the disposal of this Association it is impossible to ascertain in detail the facts as to occupation, poverty and health in the districts.   But from various sources materials are available which may serve to give some kind of picture of the conditions of the town populations.

The 1901 census returns show that out of a total of 112,854 tenements in Manchester 61,572 are of less than five rooms; and out of 45,541 tenements in Salford 27,700 are of less than five rooms.   The same returns show that nearly half the population lives in tenements of less than five rooms—264,142 people in Manchester, 106,649 in Salford.   How they are distributed and how overcrowded is shown in the tables on pp. 30 and 31.

The death-rate of a town, with due precautions, may be taken as an index of the health of its population.   Where conditions are good and the people healthy, we expect a low death-rate; where the death-rate is high we expect to find conditions detrimental to health existing.   The Registrar-General in his returns groups together 33 large towns, and in this list Manchester and Salford always appear among the half-dozen towns with the highest death-rates, although there is always a great influx of young and healthy people from the country. This indicates the prevalence of bad conditions. As stated above, the Medical Officer of Health considers that the industries carried on in the district are not, on the whole, prejudicial to the health of those employed in them; so, if he be right, we must look to other conditions. The Medical Officer suggests that insanitary conditions in and around the homes of the people and mal-nutrition, due in some cases to poverty, in other cases to ignorance, may be put among the chief causes of disease. Our experience confirms this diagnosis and, though we have perforce given most attention to insanitary conditions in this report, we consider that the poverty and the ignorance prevalent among large masses of the population require attention.

If Manchester and Salford are examined by sanitary districts it is seen that there are wide variations in the death-rates of the different districts. The table given opposite shows the death-rates for Manchester and Salford by sanitary districts for the years 1901 and 1902 : —

TABLE SHOWING AREA, DENSITY OF POPULATION AND DEATHS IN MANCHESTER AND SALFORD SANITARY DISTRICTS.

(Extracted from Reports of the Medical Officers of Health for Manchester and Salford.)

1901. Statistical Divisions.	Estimated Population.	Area in Acres.	Persons to an Acre.	Deaths. Total.	Rate per 1,000.
City of Manchester	546,408 ...	12,910 ...	42 ...	11,801 ...	21·60
I. Manchester Township	135,006 ...	1,646 ...	82 ...	3,716 ...	27·52
II. N. Manchester	167,257 ...	7,321 ...	23 ...	2,938 ...	17·57
III. S. Manchester	244,145 ...	3,943 ...	62 ...	5,147 ...	21·08
I. ⎰ Ancoats	45,014 ...	400 ...	113 ...	1,275 ...	28·32
Central	30,047 ...	748 ...	40 ...	878 ...	29·22
St. George's	59,945 ...	498 ...	120 ...	1,563 ...	26·07
I. ⎰ Cheetham	37,207 ...	919 ...	41 ...	528 ...	14·19
Crumpsall	8,852 ...	733 ...	12 ...	142 ...	16·04
Blackley	8,878 ...	1,840 ...	5 ...	139 ...	15·66
Harpurhey	15,893 ...	193 ...	82 ...	273 ...	17·18
Moston	12,161 ...	1,297 ...	9 ...	185 ...	15·21
Newton Heath	40,525 ...	1,350 ...	30 ...	712 ...	17·57
Bradford	23,766 ...	288 ...	83 ...	524 ...	22·05
Beswick	11,686 ...	96 ...	122 ...	267 ...	22·85
Clayton	8,289 ...	605 ...	14 ...	168 ...	20·27
I. ⎰ Ardwick	41,454 ...	509 ...	81 ...	865 ...	20·87
Openshaw	27,358 ...	581 ...	47 ...	552 ...	20 18
West Gorton	29,459 ...	318 ...	93 ...	562 ...	19·08
Rusholme and Kirkmanshulme	20,544 ...	1,412 ...	15 ...	391 ...	19·03
Chorlton-on-Medlock	57,956 ...	646 ...	90 ...	1,138 ...	19·64
Hulme	67,374 ...	477 ...	141 ...	1,639 ...	24·33

1902.

Statistical Divisions.	Estimated Population.	Area in Acres.	Persons to an Acre.	Deaths.	
				Total.	Rate per 1,000.
City of Manchester	550,355 ...	12,910 ...	43 ...	11,026 ...	20·03
I.　Manchester					
Township	133,590 ...	1,646 ...	81 ...	3,357 ··	25·13
II. N.　Manchester	171,925 ...	7,321 ...	23 ...	2,888 ...	17·22
III. S.　Manchester	244,840 ...	3,943 ...	63 ...	4,781 ...	19·19
I. ⎰ Ancoats	44,731 ...	400 ...	112 ...	1,130 ...	25·26
Central	29,280 ...	748 ...	39 ...	783 ...	26·74
St. George's	59,579 ...	498 ...	120 ...	1,444 ...	24·24
Cheetham	38,000 ...	919 ...	41 ...	484 ...	12·74
Crumpsall	8,955 ...	733 ...	12 ...	117 ...	13·07
Blackley	9,028 ...	1,840 ...	5 ...	149 ...	16·50
Harpurhey	16,831 ...	193 ...	87 ...	286 ...	16·99
II. ⎰ Moston	13,165 ...	1,297 ...	10 ...	176 ...	13·37
Newton Heath ....·.	41,046 ...	1,350 ...	27 ...	731 ...	19·86
Bradford	24,046 ...	288 ...	83 ...	525 ...	21·83
Beswick	11,840 ...	96 ...	123 ...	247 ...	20·86
Clayton	9,014 ...	605 ...	15 ...	173 ...	19·19
Ardwick	42,039 ...	509 ...	83 ...	805 ...	19·15
Openshaw	27,627 ...	581 ...	48 ...	513 ...	18·57
West Gorton	29,889 ...	318 ...	94 ...	505 ...	16·90
III. ⎰ Rusholme and					
Kirksmanhulme	20,841 ...	1,412 ...	18 ...	415 ...	16·55
Chorlton-on-Medlock	57,685 ...	646 ...	89 ...	1,074 ...	18·62
Hulme	66,759 ...	477 ...	140 ...	1,469 ...	22·00

1901.

Statistical Divisions.	Estimated Population.*	Area in Acres.	Persons to an Acre.	Deaths.	
				Total.	Rate per 1,000.
Salford Borough ...	221,587 ...	1,354 ...	42·6 ...	4,802 ...	21·7
Regent Road	71,435 ...	964 ...	74·8 ...	1,713 ...	24·0
Greengate	33,743 ...	390 ...	86·5 ...	971 ...	28·8
Pendleton	67,023 ...	2,430 ...	27·6 ...	1,324 ...	19·8
Broughton	49,386 ...	1,418 ...	34·6 ...	794 ...	16·1

1902.

Salford Borough ...	224,007 ...	1,354 ...	43·1 ...	4,375 ...	19·2
Regent Road	71,229 ...	964 ...	73·9 ...	1,420 ...	19·6
Greengate	33,468 ...	390 ...	85·8 ...	966 ...	28·3
Pendleton	68,935 ...	2,430 ...	28·4 ...	1,254 ...	17·9
Broughton	50,375 ...	1,418 ...	35·5 ...	735 ...	14·3

* Population is estimated to the *middle* of each year.

If reference is again made to the map with these figures in mind, it will be seen that the districts with high death-rates are those mainly occupied by the working classes, and the districts with low death-rates are either occupied by well-to-do people or are, like Blackley and Moston, only gradually receiving an urban population. The map, too, shows clearly the kinds of dwellings in the different parts of the city and it may be noted that the high death-rate accompanies the slum areas, and those other districts where there are many houses on the land and few open spaces, while the low death-rates belong to districts in which there are relatively few houses and where the houses are larger and have gardens. It is sufficient here to note the coincidence.

Further evidence of the absence of healthy conditions in Manchester may be got from the following tables, for which we are indebted to Mr. Fred Thoresby. The information has been obtained from the "Supplement to the 59th Annual Report of Births, Deaths and Marriages in England " (Part II., 1897) :—

TABLE SHOWING DEATHS OF CHILDREN UNDER FIVE YEARS OF AGE.

For the ten years, 1881—1890, the following numbers of children under five years of age died out of each 100,000 :—

	England and Wales.		Manchester.		Rural Districts.
Males	24,851	...	37,674	...	17,314
Females	21,676	...	33,677	..	14,483

c

TABLE SHOWING EXPECTATION OF LIFE.

For the ten years, 1881—1890, the average expectation of
life at birth was*:—

	England and Wales.	Manchester.	Rural Districts.
Males	43·66 years	28·78 years	51·48 years
Females	47·18 „	32·67 „	54·04 „

These tables reveal the disastrous effects of crowded cities
on the life of the people. The physical effects of bad houses
and surroundings, together with poor and insufficient feeding,
are shown even more graphically in the following tables, which
we have extracted from a report made by the Medical Officer
of the Salford School Board, Dr. J. Howson Ray, in March,
1903. The Salford School Board caused anthropometric
records to be taken of some boys in three of the schools and
the averages obtained are here shown and contrasted with the
figures given for Public School Boys (the most favoured class in
England) and for the English Artisan Class in Roberts'
"Anthropometry."

---

* Cf. the *Manchester Life Tables* by Dr. John Tatham, where a fuller
analysis of the figures will be found. On p. 34 he writes : "Looking at the
figures in another way, we may say that on an average each male child born
in Manchester Township loses 10·48 years, or 39 per cent., and each female
child 9·82 years, or 34 per cent. of the normal working period of life; the
losses in the Outlying Townships being 3·00 years, or 11 per cent. of the normal
working period for males, and 2·66 years, or 9 per cent., for females. Again
on p. 37, he writes : " Here is a population of nearly 150,000 persons paying a
tax which must be reckoned, not in pounds, shillings and pence, but in years,
months, and days—a tax amounting on the average to fully 30 per cent. of
the life-time of every member of the community. Here are men and women
entering the period of decline at an age when they ought scarcely to have
passed the prime of life. And what is particularly distressing is the thought,
that although in some respects the local conditions of life have improved within
the last half century, in other respects bad has become even worse."

TABLE SHOWING ANTHROPOMETRIC RECORDS OF SALFORD SCHOOLBOYS.

(Constructed from a report by Dr. Howson Ray, Medical Officer, Salford School Board.)

	Age.		Height.		Weight.		Chest.	Head Circumference.
	Y.	M.	Ft.	In.	St.	Lbs.	In.	In.
English Artisan Class[1]	8	0	3	9	4	1	—	—
John Street Board School, Pendleton (Average of ten boys)	8	8	3	$10\frac{1}{3}$	3	$4\frac{3}{4}$	$24\frac{3}{4}$	$20\frac{1}{2}$
Grecian Street Board School, Broughton (Average of ten boys)	8	4	3	$11\frac{1}{4}$	3	7	$24\frac{3}{4}$	$20\frac{1}{2}$
Trafford Road School (Average of twelve boys)	8	7	3	$11\frac{1}{8}$	3	$3\frac{3}{4}$	$24\frac{1}{4}$	$20\frac{1}{3}$
Public School Boys[1]	10	0	4	5	4	11	—	—
English Artisan Class[1]	10	0	4	2·5	4	10	—	—
John Street Board School (Average of ten boys)	10	7	4	$2\frac{1}{2}$	4	$0\frac{1}{4}$	$26\frac{1}{4}$	$20\frac{3}{4}$
(Average of nine boys)[2] ...	10	6	4	$1\frac{1}{2}$	3	11	$25\frac{3}{4}$	$20\frac{7}{12}$
Grecian Street Board School (Average of ten boys)	10	8	4	$3\frac{3}{4}$	4	$0\frac{1}{2}$	$25\frac{3}{4}$	$20\frac{1}{2}$
Trafford Road School (Average of ten boys)	10	6	4	$2\frac{1}{2}$	4	0	$25\frac{4}{5}$	$20\frac{3}{4}$
Public School Boys[1]	13	0	4	10·5	6	4	—	—
English Artisan Class[1]	13	0	4	7·5	5	8	—	—
John Street School (Average of ten boys)	13	5	4	$5\frac{1}{2}$	4	$5\frac{3}{4}$	$27\frac{1}{3}$	$20\frac{3}{4}$
Grecian Street Board School (Average of ten boys)	13	5	4	$9\frac{2}{5}$	5	$7\frac{3}{4}$	$28\frac{1}{2}$	$20\frac{3}{4}$
Trafford Road Board School (Average of ten boys)	13	6	4	$8\frac{3}{10}$	5	0	$28\frac{1}{5}$	$20\frac{3}{4}$

[1] These figures are from C. Roberts' *Manual of Anthropometry*. The heights are given without shoes; the weights include clothes = 9 lbs.

[2] *i.e.*, Excluding one boy of exceptionally large build, who had only recently moved into Pendleton from an outside district.

The following facts should be borne in mind in considering these tables; we quote from the report:—" The birth-rate and death-rate in the Pendleton district are higher than in the Broughton district. On the other hand, the John Street School is in a distinctly poorer neighbourhood than the Grecian Street School, and, whilst the latter school is fairly well ventilated and is adjacent to a large park, the John Street School is poorly ventilated and draws its air supply largely from the ground level, where there are narrow streets and property of a poor description. Whilst a certain amount of the improved physique of the boys at Grecian Street is probably due to a better class of home and a better class and greater quantity of food, I believe that a good deal is owing to the better ventilation of this school, to the encouragement of exercises such as swimming, and to the proximity of Albert Park, which acts as an air reservoir for the streets and houses from which the boys come. Contrast this with John Street School, and one sees a poorly ventilated building, drawing its breath from the comparatively stagnant pool of air that surrounds the premises, children coming from poor homes and with little opportunity for healthy recreation, a smoke-laden atmosphere limiting the amount of bright sunlight that should be available, and probably with insufficient and often unsuitable food. . . . . . The record for the Trafford Road School shows that this school is slightly above the mean of the John Street and Grecian Street Schools, as might be expected from the character of the school and of its surroundings."

One further observation may be made here. The notification of cases of infectious disease permits us to ascertain in which parts of the city these cases most frequently occur. In Manchester " spot " maps are prepared weekly which show approximately the locality of each case reported of certain infectious diseases. Comparison of a series of these maps shows, as might be expected, that those districts in which there are most houses to the acre, in which there are fewest open spaces, in which the houses are of the poorest description, are those in which cases of disease most frequently occur.

POVERTY.

It is difficult to gauge the amount of poverty existing in the city and borough. To ascertain the amount with precision would require an investigation similar to those undertaken by Mr. Seebohm Rowntree in York[1] and Mr. Charles Booth in London[2]. Our actual investigation of Manchester conditions has been carried out in areas selected because it was apparent that the conditions of life there were unsatisfactory, and we are consequently unable to generalise from them. In them we found conditions as bad as any reported by Mr. Rowntree or Mr. Booth.

As is well known, these observers, using somewhat different methods, and working one in the metropolis, the other in York, obtained figures respecting poverty which are nearly the same. From a close study of their works, we are convinced that an investigation in Manchester and Salford would yield very similar results. If, then, we take the percentages of poverty ascertained by Messrs. Booth and Rowntree we may calculate the number of persons in poverty in our district, and shall be justified in believing that the results give a fair picture of the case.

Mr. Charles Booth and his workers ascertained that 30·7 per cent. of the population of London were in poverty, that is, were in a greater or less degree of want. Mr. Rowntree in York found that 27·84 per cent. of the population was in poverty, and remarks that his investigation was carried on during a period of considerable prosperity, which may account for the proportion of poverty being less than that found by Mr. Booth.

The Census for 1901 gives the following populations:—

Manchester	543,872
Salford	220,957
Total	764,829

[1] "Poverty : a study of Town Life." By Seebohm Rowntree. Macmillan and Co.

[2] "The Life and Labour of the People." Edited by Charles Booth. Macmillan and Co.

The number of persons in this population living in poverty
would be—

By Mr. Booth's estimate (30·7 per cent.)   234,802
By Mr. Rowntree's estimate (27·84 per cent.)......   212,928

We may assume then that in the two towns in 1901 at
least 212,000 persons and possibly 230,000 persons were in
want. As the prices of necessaries which were rising in 1901
have continued to rise and there has been apparently a slacken-
ing in trade it is likely that now (in 1903) the higher figure
is the more accurate.

In Mr. Rowntree's work an interesting section deals with
what he calls "primary" poverty—the condition of those
whose total earnings are insufficient to enable them to obtain
the necessaries for physical efficiency.

This is ascertainable since these necessaries are shelter,
clothing and food. Basing his calculations on the researches
of Atwater and Drs. Dunlop and Paton, Mr. Rowntree
estimated the amount of money required to provide the food
needed to keep a man and his family in physical efficiency,
and, taking prices current in York for rent and clothing, he
ascertained the necessary expenditures on these and constructed
the table given below.

TABLE SHOWING THE MINIMUM NECESSARY EXPENDITURE PER
WEEK FOR FAMILIES OF VARIOUS SIZES.

Family.	Food.		Rent.		Household Sundries.		Total.	
	s.	d.	s.	d.	s.	d.	s.	d.
1 man	3	0			2	6 ...	7	0
1 woman	3	0	1	6	2	6 ...	7	0
1 man and 1 woman	6	0			3	2 ...	11	8
1 man, woman and child	8	3 ...	2	6	... 3	9 ...	14	6
„ „ 2 children	10	6 ...	4	0	... 4	4 ...	18	10
„ „ 3 „	12	9 ...	4	0	... 4	11 ...	21	8
„ „ 4 „	15	0			5	6 ...	26	0
„ „ 5 „	17	3			6	1 ...	28	10
„ „ 6 „	19	6	5	6	6	8 ...	31	8
„ „ 7 „	21	9			7	3 ...	34	6
„ „ 8 „	24	0			7	10 ...	37	4

Where the income of the household fell below the amount indicated in the table, the family was classed as being in primary poverty. This analysis of the population of York showed that 9·91 per cent. of the population were in a state of primary poverty. Applying this percentage to the Manchester and Salford population as before, we get 75,794 persons who in 1901 were living in a state of primary poverty. We have noted that the prices of necessaries have been rising since 1901, and in the table below we compare these with the prices used by Mr. Rowntree in his investigation. Rents in Manchester and Salford are higher than in York, and unless a larger proportion of heads of households get higher wages in Manchester and Salford than in York, it is obvious that poverty in our district must be more intense. So far as we have been able to ascertain there is little difference between the earnings of men engaged in the same trade in Manchester and Salford and in York.

TABLE COMPARING FOOD-PRICES IN YORK AND MANCHESTER.

	Prices in York, as given by Mr. Rowntree.	PRICES IN MANCHESTER.		
	s. d.	A s. d.	B s. d.	C† s. d.
Flour, per stone	1 4 per 12lbs.	1 4 per 12lbs.	1 4 per 12lbs.	1 3
New Milk, per pint...	0 1½ ...	0 1½ ...	0 1¾ ...	10½
Skim Milk, per pint...	0 0¾ ...	— ...	0 1 ...	—
Oatmeal, per lb.	0 2* ...	0 2 ...	0 2 ...	0 2
Dried Peas, per lb. ...	0 2¼* ...	0 2½ ...	0 2½ ...	0 2½
Bacon, per lb.	0 6 ...	0 6½ ...	0 8	4d. to 11d.
Cheese, per lb.	0 6½ ...	0 7½ ...	0 8	7d. to 9d.
Sugar, per lb.	0 1¾ ...	0 2¼ ...	0 2	1½d. to 2¾d.
Potatoes, per lb.	0 0½ per 20lbs.	1 4 per 5lbs.	0 3½ per lb.	0 1
Margarine, per lb. ...	0 8* ...	0 7½ ...	—	6d. & 8d.
Butter, per lb.	1 0	1/1 & 1/2	1 0	11d. to 1/2
Biscuits, per lb.	0 4 ...	0 4 ...	0 4	2½d. to 1/4
Cocoa, per lb.	1 0*	8d.1/- & 1/2	0 8	1/- to 1/4
Tea, per lb.	1 5 ...	1 4 ...	1 4	1/4 to 3/0
Coffee, per lb.	1 0* ...	1 2 ...	1 0	10d. to 1/8
Treacle, per lb..........	0 1¾ ...	0 1½ ...	0 2 ...	0 1½
Onions, per lb..........	0 0½ ...	0 1 ...	0 1½ ...	0 1
Yeast, per lb.	0 8 ...	0 10 ...	0 8 ...	0 10
Currants, per lb.......	0 3½ ...	0 3 ...	0 4 ...	0 3
Suet, per lb.............	0 8 ...	0 9 ...	0 8 ...	0 8

* These prices, says Mr. Rowntree, are subject to a reduction of 5 per cent., which is approximately the dividend allowed by the Co-operative Stores to ordinary purchasers.
† The figures given in this column have been obtained from a Co-operative Society: those given in column A and B were obtained from ordinary retail dealers in Ancoats and Bradford.

What primary poverty means and what is the condition of upwards of 75,000 of our fellow citizens may best be gathered from the words of Mr. Rowntree himself. " And let us clearly understand what ' merely physical efficiency' means. A family living upon the scale allowed for in this estimate must never spend a penny on railway fare or omnibus. They must never go into the country unless they walk. They must never purchase a halfpenny newspaper or spend a penny to buy a ticket for a popular concert. They must write no letters to absent children, for they cannot afford to pay the postage. They must never contribute anything to their church or chapel, or give any help to a neighbour which costs them money. They cannot save, nor can they join sick club or trade union, because they cannot pay the necessary subscriptions. The children must have no pocket money for dolls, marbles, or sweets. The father must smoke no tobacco, and must drink no beer. The mother must never buy any pretty clothes for herself or for her children, the character of the family wardrobe as for the family diet being governed by the regulation, ' Nothing must be bought but that which is absolutely necessary for the maintenance of physical health, and what is bought must be of the plainest and most economical description.' Should a child fall ill, it must be attended by the parish doctor. Finally, the wage-earner must never be absent from his work for a single day.

If any of these conditions are broken, the extra expenditure involved is met, and can only be met by limiting the diet, or, in other words, by sacrificing physical efficiency."[1]

INTEMPERANCE.

It is impossible in a survey of social conditions in Manchester and Salford to omit reference to intemperance. The description given elsewhere of the homes of some Manchester citizens may explain, if it cannot excuse, the unfortunately frequent abuse of the public-house. Where the home is overcrowded, dull and dismal, and where there are few or no

---

[1] "Poverty." By B. Seebohm Rowntree. Pp. 133, 134.

opportunities for wholesome recreation, the public-house is the only place to turn to. And ample provision of public-houses is made. In Manchester there were 486 public-houses and 2,394 beer and wine houses in 1902. On the population figures for 1901, this gives one licensed house for each 189 people of all ages, a provision which must far exceed the needs of the town. There are also many clubs at which intoxicating liquors can be obtained by members.

During 1902, the Manchester police arrested 7,114 persons for being drunk and disorderly and proceeded by summons against 294 others for the same offences; a total of 8,008. There were 1,114 persons taken into custody for other offences who were also drunk. Although these figures show a decrease from the previous year, they are still very high, and give an additional force to our plea for the provision of better dwellings and surroundings for the people. Not only are better houses needed, but more open spaces for use in summer and concerts and other entertainments for the winter months are required.

CHAPTER III.

Unwholesome Conditions Considered.

In this section of the report we propose to describe some
of the chief factors which make districts and houses unwholesome. It is of the utmost importance that every citizen should
be familiar with those defects in the arrangement of houses
on the ground, in the construction of houses, and in the usage
of houses which make them unfit for healthy life. Not only
can such knowledge be employed for the protection of the
individual citizen and his family, but it ought to be claimed
as a civic duty that the inhabitants of our city should use
their knowledge and, by reporting to the sanitary authorities
instances of defective structure or bad usage of the kind to be
described, help to protect and improve the public health. The
illustrations of the conditions described have all been drawn
from Manchester and Salford.

Overcrowding.

It would be unnecessary to define *overcrowding* if the
word were not used in a technical sense. The distribution of
population is usually stated with regard to area as so many
persons per acre or per square mile and with regard to cubic
space as, in the census returns, so many persons per house or
per room.

But in the discussion of overcrowding we are hampered
by the fact that no authoritative standards have been established or more accurately no exact authoritative standards.
For density on area there is no official standard at all. The
late Sir B. W. Richardson has stated that to insure healthy
life to its citizens the maximum density of a city should be
25 persons to an acre. It is idle to demand at present the
adoption of such a standard in our towns, though much might
be said for enforcing it in the suburban districts by which the
town is increasing. The density in all of the statistical

divisions of Manchester and Salford has already been given in the table on pp. 17 and 18.

It has long been noticed that a high density per acre is usually accompanied by a high death rate and a high zymotic disease rate. Manchester and Salford do not provide exceptions to this general statement. It is seen further, as we have already noted, that the districts with the highest density are those mainly occupied by the poorer parts of our city populations.

Overcrowding of cubic space is usually measured by the census standard of more than two people to a room. The absence of exactitude in this standard, owing to the variations in the size of rooms, and the absence of any definition of what constitutes a room, is obvious. It is obvious also that the harm caused by such overcrowding must to some extent be dependent on the age of those inhabiting the rooms, and also on their relationship, the structural state of the house, and especially on the degree in which it is ventilated.

The amount of overcrowding, judged by census standard, in Manchester and Salford is comparatively low. But much overcrowding exists, and not infrequently gross instances are to be found. The census figures for 1901, given in the accompanying table, show the overcrowding in houses of different sizes, and speak for themselves. The statistics to the right of the thick vertical lines are statistics of overcrowding.

OVERCROWDING.

City of Manchester.—Statistics of Houses and Occupants from 1901 Census.

Total Tenements, 112,854.

Population, 543,872.

Tenements less than 5 rooms, 61,572.

Rooms.	Tenements.	Persons to a house.											
		1	2	3	4	5	6	7	8	9	10	11	12 or more.
1	2,140	820	870	318	87	28	10	2	1	3	—	—	1
2	6,869	871	1884	1591	1197	771	331	148	56	9	9	2	—
3	4,994	192	871	997	933	774	576	359	174	82	22	7	7
4	47,569	938	6787	8939	9083	7542	5885	3877	2429	1231	574	185	99

450	1-roomed houses are overcrowded, containing	1,553 persons.
1,326	2-roomed ,, ,, ,,	7,518 ,,
651	3-roomed ,, ,, ,,	5,024 ,,
2,089	4-roomed ,, ,, ,,	20,042 ,,
4,516		34,137 ,, live in overcrowded houses in Manchester.

OVERCROWDING.

Salford (Borough) Statistics of Houses and Occupants from 1901 Census.

Total Tenements, 45,541.

Population, 220,957.

Tenements less than 5 rooms, 27,700.

Rooms.	Tenements.	Persons to a house.											
		1	2	3	4	5	6	7	8	9	10	11	12 or more.
1	807	314	286	119	70	9	7	2	—	—	—	—	—
2	3,491	345	838	753	669	430	268	119	46	15	7	—	1
3	2,212	59	297	431	405	371	294	192	92	37	26	4	4
4	18,190	294	2530	3376	3484	2960	2257	1553	906	485	222	87	36

207 1-roomed houses are overcrowded, containing 738 persons.
886 2-roomed ,, ,, 5,176 ,,
355 3-roomed ,, ,, 2,765 ,,
830 4-roomed ,, ,, 7,974 ,,
————
2,278   16,653 ,, live in overcrowded houses in Salford.

But when we leave statistical tables and measure some of the houses we find matters look worse. The amount of air space in a room may be taken as its cubic content. In the Model Bye-laws of the Local Government Board, 400 cubic feet of air space is required for every person over ten years of age in any room not exclusively used as a sleeping apartment, and 200 cubic feet for children under ten years. In rooms used exclusively for sleeping the amounts are 300 and 150 respectively. But the Army Regulations require 600 cubic feet per head in barracks, the Metropolitan Police require 450, the Poor Law requires 500 cubic feet. It has to be remembered that to keep the air pure and uncontaminated a system of ventilation much more perfect than is found even in better class houses is required. Physiologists have put human requirements at 880 cubic feet of fresh air every hour. To change the air in a small room completely every hour, which would be the practical application of the statement quoted, would cause an uncomfortable draught, so we are forced to the conclusion that rooms must be made bigger and the air be changed gradually.

A few illustrations will show the conditions under which some families live. Many other examples might be quoted, all emphasising the same point. As we have shown above, the Local Government Board standard, with which we make comparisons, is a low estimate of the required air space.

No. 61, C—— Street is a four-roomed house with a small scullery, occupied by a family of four adults and four children. The living room, which also serves as a bedroom for one of the adults, has a cubic content of 954 feet. By the Local Government Board bye-laws aforementioned the family should have a living room with a cubic content of 2,400 feet.

No. 39, C—— Street consists of two rooms, one used as a bedroom for three adults (two men and one woman) having a cubic content of 875 feet. From this has to be taken the space occupied by beds and furniture.

No. 15, S—— Street is a back-to-back house, consisting of two rooms, and occupied by husband and wife, wife's mother and three children under 14. The cubic contents of each room are 990 feet. The living room has one sleeper, the bedroom is occupied by the father and mother and their three children. By Local Government Board standards this room should have a cubic capacity of 1,050 cubic feet.

No. 27, S—— Street, a back-to-back house, has two adults and three children sleeping in one bedroom with a cubic content of 990 feet.

No. 10, B—— S—— Street, a back-to-back house with two rooms, is occupied by two adults and four children. The bedroom, with a cubic content of 733 feet, is used for a workroom (sewing) and washing. The living room—1,046 cubic feet—is living room and sleeping place too for the six inmates. By Local Government Board standards the requirements would be 1,600 cubic feet.

Other examples of overcrowding are given in the investigator's notes printed in Chapter IV.

STRUCTURAL DEFECTS.—THE KIND OF DWELLING.

The kinds of dwellings found in the districts of Manchester and Salford mainly occupied by the working classes may be considered in four groups:—(1) "through" cottages, (2) "back-to-back" houses, (3) "tenement" houses, and (4) "block dwellings."

"Block dwellings" (commonly called "barrack" dwellings) are principally represented in Manchester and Salford by the blocks built by the Corporations on sites formerly occupied by insanitary dwellings. A large block in Ancoats, owned by a company, was obtained by the conversion of an old mill. There are a few other blocks, but this type is rare, and of recent origin in this district. A block of "flat" houses may be regarded as a row of cottages built vertically, each house being complete in itself or sharing sanitary accommodation and the like with its immediate neighbours on the flat. Although this type is the usual form of dwelling in Scottish and many continental cities, and is rapidly becoming common in London, it is not a popular type in English towns. It is felt by tenants that they lose to some extent the privacy of their homes, that they are thrown into close contact with their neighbours whether they will or not, and there is often an objection to climbing stairs.

The building of blocks of flat dwellings by our Corporations and by others is a matter which is discussed elsewhere (see p. 84) in this report. Here we are mainly concerned to note the effect of certain types of dwelling on the health of the community. In the well-built and carefully supervised dwellings referred to above, a marked change has taken place in the death rate as compared with the death rates of the old insanitary property formerly covering the sites, and from this point of view the dwellings are a real gain to the community. The figures given in the official reports show a reduction in the death-rate, in the case of the Oldham Road Dwellings of 39 per cent., and in the case of the Pollard Street Dwellings of 36 per cent.

" TENEMENT " HOUSES.

By " tenement " houses are meant houses of several storeys, built originally for one family, but now occupied by two or more. Houses of this type are not very common in Manchester and Salford, but especially in one district many are to be found. The part of Manchester lying between Shudehill, Victoria Station, Ludgate Hill, and Rochdale Road contains many old houses evidently built to accommodate a single family each but now sometimes having a family to each room.

Referring to houses used in this way Dr. Sykes, Medical Officer of Health for St. Pancras, says:—" It may be concluded that in the old type of vertical dwelling-houses constructed for one family, the morbidity and mortality tend to increase in direct ratio with the increase in the number of dwellings in the houses, the decrease in the number of rooms in the dwellings, and the increase of the number of persons in the rooms."

Thus in a four-roomed house originally intended for one family, the danger of the occupants falling victims to disease, and of fatal results from disease, increases when the house is let as two two-roomed houses, and still further increases when it is let as four one-roomed houses. This danger is also increased by every increase in the number occupying the separate rooms.

A few examples from the investigator's papers are given below:—

No. 37, —— Street. A two-storeyed house has four rooms and a scullery. Four families occupy it at present, each family consisting of two adults and a child. One water-tap and sink contained in the scullery (which measures 9ft. by 6ft. by 8ft.) serve all four families. The observer notes that the house is very dirty. One pail closet in the street serves for this house and the two neighbouring houses, which each contain two families.

No. 12, —— Street has three rooms and contains two families, one of five individuals, another of four. The house has no water-tap of its own; the occupants use a tap in an entry behind the house which is common to *six* houses, and a closet used by *two* other houses. This house is kept clean.

No. 1, —— Street (typical of others in the street), is a five-roomed house occupied by four families (10 persons). Five houses share the closet used by the inmates of this house and 22 houses the water-tap, which is in the street. The house and tenants are described as very dirty.

" BACK-TO-BACK " HOUSES.

It is now fortunately impossible to build back-to-back houses in our district, and much has been done in recent years to remove these unwholesome dwellings from our midst. Nevertheless a surprisingly large number of such houses is to be found, as a reference to our key map will show.

STREET.

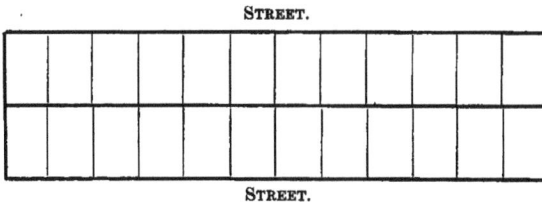

STREET.

PLAN OF A BLOCK OF " BACK-TO-BACK " HOUSES.

d

A back-to-back house is one in which there is only one open face, *i.e.*, the outside air only reaches a small part of the house. Such houses are usually only one room deep, and therefore have as many storeys as there are rooms. Examples have been quoted (see p. 59) in which there are two rooms on a floor, the back room getting its light and air through the front room. In back-to-back houses there is no possibility of obtaining a through current of air without which it is impossible to thoroughly ventilate a house. Much attention has been given by Dr. Tatham, Dr. Niven, and other authorities on public health matters to the mortality of the occupants of back-to-back houses. It has been shown by these observers that the rate of mortality from all causes is higher among the dwellers in back-to-back houses than among the same classes living in "through" houses, and the death rates from pulmonary disease, phthisis and zymotic diseases is also higher. This in itself should be sufficient reason for pressing forward the total abolition of houses of this type.

But there are some other reasons for wishing to hasten the departure of the back-to-back house. A back-to-back house means no yard. Sanitary conveniences have, therefore, to be provided either in the court on which the houses look or in the street. Of both arrangements examples have been given in the descriptions of districts (see p. 51). In one case, the closets stand in a court. There are five closets in the block; they are usually in a filthy condition, and certainly not more than two of them are fit for use. What such arrangements entail can, however, be better gathered from our illustrations. The first illustration shows one side of a row of back-to-back houses with the closets entered from the street. These closets were found in a filthy condition, standing open to all comers. Incidentally it may be noticed that in this last illustration, the closet adjoins the living room and is under the bedroom of one house. In another row of back-to-back houses examined, it was found that the smells from the closet made the room above uninhabitable, yet the house was let and occupied.

In St. Michael's Ward. Back-to-back houses. Note closets in middle of block, beside woman standing on pavement.

In Ancoats. A row of back-to-back houses. Note tap, closets and ashplace, the latter immediately under a bedroom.

To face p. 36.

It is not surprising that decent and modest people shrink from using conveniences of this kind, probably with evil results to their health. Nor is it surprising to find that the manners of those who live in such conditions and accept them are coarse.

Frequently the water supply of back-to-back houses is poor. A tap in the street, whence all water has to be fetched, is all the provision made. We have found instances in which six, eight, ten, twenty, and even twenty-six houses were dependent on one tap. From what has been said of the difficulty of ventilating back-to-back houses and of the ascertained fact that disease has more frequently fatal results in these houses, it is obvious that a good and accessible water supply, which would give every encouragement to cleanliness, is for them especially a desideratum of the first importance.

" THROUGH " HOUSES.

The " through " house is distinguished from the back-to-back house by having at least two faces in contact with the open air. The familiar cottage which lines so many miles of our streets in Manchester and Salford is of this type. When well-planned, well-built, and kept in good repair, with ample air space around it, this type of house seems to be the most suitable for healthy life. But the conditions must be observed. It is not unfair to say that few houses in Manchester and Salford occupied by the working classes are well-planned. There are not a few examples to be found of houses, even of recent erection, which are not well-built. Often, too, the narrowness of the streets and of the space between the backs of the houses, together with the long unbroken rows, makes it impossible to have an ample air supply. Finally, examples of lack of repair are to be found in abundance.

Houses are badly planned which do not give the inmates the possibility of making the fullest and best use of the space. In the case of hundreds of houses in Manchester and Salford the house has two rooms downstairs and two upstairs. The upstairs rooms are generally bedrooms; the back room (though sometimes the front room) downstairs is kitchen and living room, and generally some attempt is made to keep the other downstairs room as a parlour. The result is that the family overcrowds during the day a room in which cooking, washing, etc., are carried on, and in which the children play, and then often overcrowds two bedrooms at night. In the latter case, overcrowding is not the only evil. The children, even when grown up and of different sexes, have to share the same room, a state of affairs which cannot be regarded as desirable. In the section of the report dealing with the erection of new houses, we have indicated our views on the planning of houses.

DAMPNESS AND COLDNESS.

Faults in building show themselves in various ways. Hurriedly and cheaply built property is nearly always found to be cold and damp. Dampness may be due to wetness of the soil or subsoil, hence the importance of seeing that these are well drained. Sometimes a house is damp owing to water rising through the walls from the soil or percolating from the roof. Examples of houses which suffer from this last defect have been found. The roof has been allowed to get into a state of disrepair; rain soaks through the ceiling and down the bedroom walls and the atmosphere becomes laden with moisture. That dampness is inimical to health is well-known, but it may be well to point out that it has been conclusively shown that attention to the proper draining of the soil and to keeping houses dry has had a marked effect in reducing the prevalence of phthisis, a disease which is given as the cause of death in 1902 of 652 persons in Manchester and 380 in Salford.

Here are some remarks from the visitors' note-books:—

No. 7, —— Street. "House in very bad condition. Walls and ceilings damp and falling. This house has five rooms and is occupied by four families—15 individuals."

No. 1, —— Street. "House very old and damp. Very dirty house and tenants. House smells."

No. 9, —— Street. "Walls and ceiling damp. Landlord seems unwilling to keep house in repair."

No. 10, —— Street. " Back kitchen and living room very damp. Sanitary authority has requested landlord to attend to repairs and drains."

No. 14, —— Street. " Walls of rooms and floors very damp."

No. 9, —— Place. " House terribly damp and back bedroom walls literally wet; rain comes in and makes bed damp. Every pane broken. Tenant seems inclined to be negligent, but has no encouragement to keep house tidy owing to bad state of house."

No. 10, —— Street. " Part of stair wall and bedroom wall damp and falling in."

No. 20, —— Street. " Two-roomed house. Invalid child in bed in bedroom, which is very damp. Water dripping from ceiling on to bed and floor. Wet patches in walls."

Coldness is a characteristic which frequently accompanies dampness. Unseasoned woodwork used in the construction of a house soon shrinks and allows cold air to enter. In jerry built houses or in houses in bad repair coldness is due to the flimsiness of the walls. Dr. Sykes remarks in this connection: " The coldness and dampness within the dwelling are not only injurious themselves, but indirectly they lead to the closure of all openings and the stagnation of air in order to obtain more warmth."

Due provision for ventilation should also be made in every house which is to be occupied. In the course of our investigations we have found windows which would not open. Sometimes the tenants admitted that they had fastened the windows, but in other cases apparently the window had never been openable. It is true that the means of ventilation are often not used by the tenants. One may pass along street after street at night-time without finding a bedroom window open, but it ought to be possible to ventilate thoroughly every room of every house. We have been assured by an experienced Medical Officer of Health that but for the bad building of many houses erected in the past, which has allowed fresh air to enter freely, there would have been even more disease in our towns than there has been. No great improvement in health seems

to be possible in our towns till all houses are much more fully
ventilated than most houses are at present.

Occasionally houses are allowed to get into a state of
disrepair which makes them a danger to life and limb. We
have seen houses in which the staircases were rotten, wanting
steps and entirely unsafe. We have visited a house where an
incautious visitor might fall through into a coal depôt below.
While this report has been taking its final form, the collapse
of three houses in Ancoats, causing loss of life, has drawn
attention to the dangers of disrepair.

Frequent references to the state of disrepair will be found
in the remarks column of the investigator's notes, printed in
the next chapter.

DARKNESS OF ROOMS.

Only in recent years has attention been drawn to the
importance of securing adequate lighting in houses. Even in
the houses being built to-day, and still more in houses built
when bye-laws were more lax or before building bye-laws had
been framed, enough importance is not given to the proper
lighting of rooms. In towns such as ours, where the air is
almost always charged with smoke and dust, it is difficult
enough to get sunshine, but when we allow houses to be built
on each side of narrow streets, or round narrow courts, or in
the shadow of great factories and warehouses, and when these
houses have small windows, and, finally, when the tenants stop
the entrance of the light available by curtains and blinds, there
can be little hope of healthy life. Our building bye-laws
now prevent the erection of houses under such conditions, but
too many of the inhabited houses in the poorer parts of our
towns would be unwholesome if they had no other defect than
the existing darkness of their rooms. " Darkness is known to
cause anæmia and to retard the development of animals, and
the younger the animal is the greater the effects." Will any-
one who has seen the anæmic faces and stunted forms of the
dwellers say that lack of sunshine is not one of the greatest
defects in our city.

In Ardwick. Houses which are beginning to want careful repairs. Roofs defective : let in water.

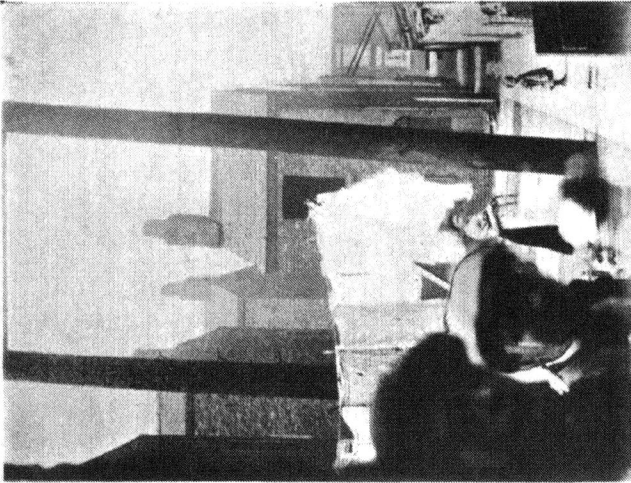

In Chorlton-on-Medlock. A crowded area. Note signs of disrepair.

To face p. 40.

"Direct sunshine, and even diffused daylight, warms and dries, sets up air currents, removes stagnant air, dissipates humidity, resolves unstable compounds and conduces to cleanliness, and the absence of light produces opposite results," says Dr. Sykes. And again he adds:—"Briefly, the indications of experiment and observation are that the healthiness of the dwelling in this country increases in proportion to the amount of daylight and sunlight admitted. The day lighting of habitable rooms should be such as to enable reading, writing, and sewing to be carried on with facility."[1] If rooms which are not so lighted are not habitable, then scores of rooms in Manchester and Salford ought to be closed.

It has been ascertained by bacteriologists that the omnipresent disease germs are killed by exposure to direct sunlight. This is another reason for seeing that our houses are flooded with light if possible. Dr. Ransome, speaking at the Jubilee Conference of the Salford Sanitary Association in 1902, quoted the following striking instance illustrating the difference between conditions in Ancoats and the suburbs. We give Dr. Ransome's words:—"Many years ago I pointed out that there were certain districts in Ancoats where the sputum of consumptives could exist for many months and retain its virulence, while at the same time that identical sputum, in a comparatively short period, entirely lost its power of reproducing the disease in my own house in Bowdon. A house thoroughly well ventilated and well lighted is practically a safe place, even if there are consumptives dwelling in it, if they take proper care in dealing with the material."

Incidentally the investigators mention many cases of dark rooms, though as a rule no note has been made unless the light was greatly obscured.

In —— Court, the houses are dark owing partly to the smallness of the windows, partly to the nearness of high buildings.

In —— Street, four houses are very dark owing to the obstruction of light by neighbouring houses.

----

[1] "Public Health and Housing," by Dr. Sykes, p. 72.

In —— Street, rooms are dark owing to nearness of high wall and house.

In —— Place, rooms dark owing to nearness of a wall and opposite houses. " A high wall rises within three feet of back door making kitchen dark."

The high infantile mortality in some parts of Manchester and Salford inhabited by the poorer working classes is mentioned in the reports of the Medical Officers of Health.

The following figures are from the report by Dr. Niven on the Health of Manchester : —

TABLE SHOWING PROPORTION OF DEATHS UNDER ONE YEAR.
Per 1,000 Births.

District.	1898.	1899.	1900.	1901.	1902.	Average for 1898– 1902.
Ancoats	208	240	213	234	178	214
Central	253	239	244	255	139	226
St. George's	211	246	226	231	173	217
Newton Heath	173	196	167	196	151	176
Bradford	212	225	209	200	165	205
Beswick	154	169	181	203	167	174
Clayton	185	224	182	304	173	213
Ardwick	205	215	186	188	158	190
Openshaw	220	216	190	211	159	199
Gorton (West)	217	216	191	190	148	192
Chorlton-on-Medlock	193	215	190	184	138	184
Hulme	197	196	199	222	160	194

The following figures are taken from a table in the report of Dr. Tattersall on the health of Salford in 1902 : —

TABLE SHOWING PROPORTION OF DEATHS UNDER ONE YEAR.
Per 1,000 Births.

District.	1898.	1899.	1900.	1901.	1902.	Average for 1898– 1902.
Borough of Salford	213	211	208	205	157	198
Regent Road	230	248	236	238	172	224
Greengate	225	209	224	246	178	216
Pendleton	207	177	192	190	147	182
Broughton	180	198	171	139	130	163

In Chorlton-on-Medlock. A narrow street. Houses dark.

In Ardwick. This house and others in same line only six feet from railway arches. Rooms dark.

To face p. 42.

These figures show the proportion for *all births* (illegitimate as well as legitimate). The mortality among illegitimate children is much higher, but the proportion given would only be slightly reduced if the figures were confined to legitimate births.

Sir James Crichton Browne, in discussing the causes of infantile mortality, asserts that the chief causes are (1) the prevalence of overcrowding and other insanitary conditions, including especially the absence of sunshine and fresh air, (2) prenatal causes, due to the poverty of the parents, and (3) improper feeding of infants. We do not seek to minimise the other causes, but think it right to emphasise the untoward influences of lack of light and air.

Other defects in houses which must be mentioned in this chapter are the absence of water supply, the absence of closets or unsatisfactory closet accommodation, the absence of means of disposing of house refuse, ashes, etc., and the absence of sufficient air space about the house.

WATER SUPPLY.

The points of importance in a water supply are that the water be pure, sufficient in quantity and accessible to the users. In Manchester and Salford we can claim that the first two conditions are complied with; but the records given in the following pages of the investigation of typical districts show that much might be done to improve the accessibility of the supply. No city sanitary authority would now allow houses to be erected in which at least one water tap for every two houses was not provided. But what we have seen is that in many streets a single tap has to meet the requirements of all the houses in the street. Such a tap cannot be equally accessible to all the houses, and some tenants must carry all the water they need a considerable distance. We use water freely in modern houses for cleansing purposss, when the only labour is that of turning a tap, or at most of carrying the water from one room to another. But if we imagine ourselves for a moment in the position of the tenants in the cases quoted below, having to leave our house every time water is required and then having to carry it some considerable distance, we can understand how hard we make it for such tenants to keep themselves and their houses clean.

Here are a few examples : —

WATER SUPPLY IN SOME MANCHESTER STREETS.

We	have	once	found	40	houses	sharing	one	tap.
,,		once	,,	30		,,		,,
,,		once	,,	26		,,		,,
,,		once	,,	22		,,		,,
,,		twice	,,	20		,,		,,
,,		once	,,	16		,,		,,
,,	.	once	,,	15		,,		,,
,,		once	,,	12		,,		,,
,,		once	,,	11		,,		,,
,,	six	times	,,	10		,,		,,
,,		thrice	,,	9		,,		,,
,,	five	times	,,	8		,,		,,
,,		twice	,,	7		,,		,,
,,		twice	,,	6		,,		,,
,,		twice	,,	5		,,		,,

Where so many houses are without a water supply, it is perhaps superfluous to note that few working men's houses have baths, and that, in many cases, there are no appliances for washing clothes. It is, however, certain that a constantly increasing proportion of new houses built for occupation by the working classes are provided with baths and conveniences for washing clothes. Even in the poorer and older districts, municipal baths and washhouses partially meet the needs of the community. The proposal put forward by the Ladies' Public Health Society, that baths should be established by the municipality in cottage houses in the poorer districts is worthy of careful consideration.

SANITARY CONVENIENCES.

To ensure healthy life, every house occupied should be provided with suitable sanitary conveniences. A closet ·is suitable when it is easily accessible and private to the occupants of the house and is provided with a rapid and cleanly method of removing the excreta. In a large city, where houses are closely packed together, the water-closet is, without doubt, the

In St. Michael's Ward. A group of closets on street. Water supply for 22 houses from tap, on which little girl is leaning.

A typical court in Chorlton-on-Medlock. Common water supply for six houses.

In a Salford court. These closets are for eleven houses; only one usable. All living rooms look on these. See p. 69.

In a Salford court. Some of the houses which use closets shown above.

To face p. 45.

only wholly suitable arrangement; ashes and other refuse should have a special receptacle. It should be noted in passing that the water-closet is only suitable when properly used, and experience has shown that the substitution of water-closets for simpler arrangements in poor districts does not work well unless the tenants are warned as to the need for care in using them.

In Manchester and Salford we are far from having separate closet accommodation for each house, and still further from having a universal system of water-closets. The Superintendent of the Cleansing Department in Manchester reported, on April 15th, 1902, that, within the city, there were:—Pail-closets, 73,915; midden-privies, 20,532; wet middens, 10,598; dry middens, 740; and water-closets, 45,686.

It is right to explain that the Sanitary Committee is taking steps to have pail-closets replaced by water-closets, and that year by year a considerable number of changes are made. But this change, like others, will only proceed rapidly when public opinion demands it, and, as yet, public opinion is silent on the matter. Medical authorities have pointed out that certain diseases, for example typhoid fever, occur more frequently in houses with privies than in houses with pail-closets, and more frequently in houses with pail-closets than in houses with water-closets.

Dr. P. Boobyer, Medical Officer of Health for Nottingham, gives, in his report for 1897, the following statistics:—During the ten years, 1887—96, the proportional annual incidence of typhoid fever cases in midden-privy houses was one case in 37 houses, in pail-closet houses one in 120, and in water-closet houses one case in 558 houses—that is, the incidence upon houses with privies was more than three times as great as that upon houses with pail-closets, and that upon houses with pail-closets more than four and a half times greater than that upon houses with water-closets.[1]

Not only do Manchester and Salford suffer from the prevalence of conveniences unsatisfactory in themselves, but the conditions are often made much worse by the inadequacy

---

[1] Public Health and Housing, by Dr. Sykes, p. 79, et. seq.

of the provision of these conveniences. The following table
exhibits the state of affairs. In many cases where several
closets are provided in a block for a number of houses (as is
frequently the case in rows of back-to-back houses and in some
courts) it is found that several of them are unfit for use, and
the number of families dependent on one convenience is
therefore increased.

HOUSES SHARING ONE CLOSET.

In 4 cases, eight houses share one closet.
,, 4   ,,   seven   ,,   ,,
,, 5   ,,   six   ,,   ,,
,, 13   ,,   five   ,,   ,,
,, 29   ,,   four   ,,   ,,

In one instance a block of 40 houses was investigated which
had six pail-closets for all the houses. In another instance 26
houses shared five closets, three of which were unusable. Again
19 houses were found sharing five closets. In another part of
the report we have referred to the fact that in some districts
houses are tenanted by several families. In some instances
this makes the lack of adequate closet accommodation even more
noticeable. We may quote, as an illustration, three houses,
one containing four rooms and two containing three rooms
each, which share one closet. These houses contained eight
families (30 persons) at the time they were visited.

Examples of three and two houses sharing one closet are
too numerous to quote.

With unsatisfactory closet accommodation usually goes
unsatisfactory provision for the disposal of ashes and refuse.
If it is necessary for a tenant to carry refuse far to put it in an
ashpit, there will be a tendency to allow refuse to accumulate
in the house and then to deposit it in the nearest available
place, i.e., the court or street. In several cases where more
than one house uses the same ashpit the accommodation is
insufficient, or the ashpit is not emptied frequently enough,
or it is kept in poor repair. From all of these causes refuse
and ashes tend to get scattered in the streets and courts and,
of course, are carried thence into the houses to make more dirt.

In Chorlton-on-Medlock. Old property in bad repair. Dirty street.

In St. Michael's Ward. A court with eleven houses. Note tap, closets and ash boxes. Closet doors torn from their hinges.

To face p. 46.

In Salford. A back street. Note ashpits without doors. All ashpits in this street in same condition. See p. 69.

In Ancoats. "The yards are small and the passages between the yards are very narrow." See p. 47.

Under the conditions of modern city life the only system which is quite satisfactory is that of having a portable bin, emptied at frequent intervals, and so placed that spilt refuse can readily be seen.

Insufficient Air Space about the House.

We have already spoken of the need of ample air space within the houses if healthy conditions are to prevail. But it has to be remembered that the air within the houses has constantly to be renewed from the outside air, and it is therefore of the first importance that the outside air should be fresh, and that it should come freely in contact with the house. Where streets are narrow and are arranged on a rectangular plan there is a constant tendency for air to stagnate. The wider the street the fresher will be the air in that street. Many of the parts of Manchester which were built in the earlier part of last century have streets which are too narrow to allow this free circulation of the air. And what is true of the street is even more applicable to the backs. In these older districts—we leave back-to-back houses out of account for the moment—the yards are small and the passages between the yards of houses facing two parallel streets are very narrow. In these dismal regions air stagnates. The back yards tend to become lumber places and litter heaps; the passages get strewn with refuse, and the air which reaches the house is contaminated.

In these older districts, and still too frequently in new districts, examples of long unbroken rows of houses are to be found. Such long rows again prevent the free circulation of the air about the houses.

It will not be easy to remove defects of this kind already existing in our towns. They are mainly results of the wrong laying out of ground plans. The lesson is rather that we should carefully look to the laying out of streets in districts which are not at present built upon, taking care that many of the streets shall be wide, that there shall be ample space behind the houses, and also that at intervals in the district open spaces of some size shall be left in which, if at all possible, trees and flowers may be grown to further freshen the air.

We shall again refer to planning in another chapter, but what we have said above suggests mention of another defect in the air surrounding houses. A town under present conditions cannot help having a smoky and polluted atmosphere. But with care the atmosphere might be greatly improved in this respect. It is a sad comment on our Manchester atmosphere that it has been said that trees and plants cannot flourish here. The atmospheric impurities which destroy the health of the plants cannot fail to injuriously affect the health of the human beings who live in the district. Trees and plants, too, are important factors in contributing to the healthiness of a town since they tend to restore the balance to the composition of the atmosphere by removing gaseous impurities and returning health-giving and essential oxygen.

We consider the absence of trees from our streets a matter worthy of attention. The value of vegetation is so great, from a moral as much as from a physical point of view, that we venture to suggest an imitation of Liverpool, which has slum districts much like our own. There in the wider streets of the poorer districts trees in tubs are placed, as is done here in some of the open places in town. There are several streets in Ancoats, in Hulme, and in Chorlton-on-Medlock wide enough to allow this to be done.

The pollution of the atmosphere in our towns by coal smoke has for long presented a grave problem to sanitary reformers. Thanks to efficient inspection and modern appliances, the nuisance has been greatly abated so far as factories are concerned. But there still remain thousands of smoky house chimneys. A simple inexpensive grate which would consume its own smoke is much needed. A further reduction in the price of gas and the introduction of economical and low-priced cooking and heating gas-stoves would also greatly assist in getting a pure atmosphere for Manchester and Salford.

Another defect, which is reported in a large number of houses, is the absence of any place for the storage of food. It is probably true that in the houses instanced above, where overcrowding and other insanitary conditions prevail, it seldom happens that the tenants have food to keep for any length of time, but food kept even from one meal-time to the next under such conditions must be unwholesome. In every house there should be a properly constructed food cupboard, ventilating to the outer air.

A Note on Streets.

Incidentally we have referred to the narrow streets which are common to the districts investigated. Very wide streets are infrequent in Manchester even in the centre of the city. The difficulty of getting room for two tram lines must have made this very apparent recently. But in the poorer residential districts, it is quite easy to find scores of streets only 24 feet wide or less. In the districts described, there are streets measuring only 15 feet across, and two streets are 9 feet 2 inches and 9 feet 4 inches respectively. These very narrow streets have the prefix "Back" to their names, but all the same they contain the front entrances to several houses.

The importance of the street is well put in a recent American report on housing conditions in Chicago:—" The streets and alleys are to the people of a well-to-do district only a convenience for transit. In an overcrowded district there is little else more important to the happiness and welfare of the people. For the children the alleys are playgrounds. They also assure, by their open spaces, light and ventilation to the houses. If they are clean they serve this purpose to the comfort and satisfaction of many, but if they are foul and covered with undisturbed filth they detract from, rather than add to, the healthiness and well-being of the community. Streets, even more than alleys, serve the purpose of playgrounds and open spaces. In the evenings, when the weather permits, these places swarm with the people from the neighbouring overcrowded houses.

This common property in the districts where it serves as little more than a convenience is given some care, while in the districts where it is a vital necessity it is wretchedly neglected."

How well this description of American conditions suits

our own, those who know the poorer parts of our towns can testify.

There are three points in connection with the streets to which we wish to draw attention. The first we have already mentioned, the streets are in most cases too narrow. Even with the low two-storey buildings, it is difficult to get sunshine to the houses if the street is only 24 feet wide. And narrow streets also mean little air. The air gets caught between the houses and stagnates there. Our bye-laws make it compulsory to form new streets 36 feet wide, but even that is not enough. The principal streets in every new district should be made 60 feet wide, with 36 feet or more for most of the side streets, to ensure a plentiful supply of light and air to the houses.

We do not suggest that all streets should be made wide. German experience has proved that this has the effect of unnecessarily raising rents by making the cost to builders greater. But every house should have a wide street near it to serve both as a channel for fresh air and as a place of exercise and recreation.

The next point is the paving of the streets. With the exception of a few streets in the centre of the city which have wood paving, our streets are paved with stone setts. In the business parts of the towns and along the main lines of communication this is probably necessary owing to the heavy traffic. In the poorer districts it is noticeable that the paving is often less well done and is not kept in as good repair as in the principal streets. In these districts there is little or no heavy traffic passing through the streets, so that the stone setts are not necessary. A New York Commission, appointed in 1894 to consider the housing of the poorest in the town, made a careful study of the kinds of paving most suitable for the streets in the poorer districts, and recommended the municipality to extend as quickly as possible the system of asphalt paving. The reasons for giving this advice are to be found in the following extract from the report of the Commission : —

" It would seem that this style of pavement (asphalt) is

the easiest to keep clean owing to its smoothness. Traffic through the streets on which tenement houses are built is not, as a rule, heavy enough to require the more solid pavement of stone. In the latter pavement, while it will stand more heavy trucking than any other, there are small cracks or interstices between the granite blocks, and in these dirt and other matter lodges in such a manner as to prevent the mechanical sweeps from removing them. Most of the material found in street sweepings, especially in tenement districts, is composed of animal and vegetable matter, containing micro-organisms of pathogenic character. Not only can asphalt pavement be thoroughly swept, but when necessary, as in cases of threatened epidemic, it may be washed as clean as the floor of a house. Absence of noise is one the greatest advantages of the system, especially in the more crowded tenement house districts."

We consider that the lesson of this extract might well be applied to many of our streets. The same lesson is taught by the experience of Cologne, an account of which is given in the Supplementary Volume.

The third point bears a close relation to the preceding one; it is the dirtiness of the streets. In the poorer districts the dirt and dust of the streets must be a constant source of danger to health. Most of the houses open straight from the street and every gust of wind and everyone entering the house bring a fresh supply of dirt. Where the people are not especially careful and clean, they regard the struggle with dirt as hopeless and frankly give it up, with ill effects to themselves and even more to their children. Wherever the streets are habitually dirty, one finds that the people use the street as a receptacle for garbage and rubbish, a habit strengthened doubtless by the frequent absence of proper places in which to put such material.

We cannot expect the narrow streets to be widened at once, nor can we hope that they will be at an early date paved in a more suitable way, but we do urge that steps should be taken to see that the streets in the poorer parts get as much attention

as those in the well-to-do districts. Sweeping in the smaller
streets and in the courts is not enough; they ought to be
washed down regularly. In Glasgow, which is deservedly
regarded as a model in many respects, great attention is given
to washing the streets, and to encourage cleanliness the
Corporation places, free of cost, hose connections in all private
streets and courts. We hope that so soon as our water supply
admits, a similar system will be established here and measures
be taken to see that it is used.

CHAPTER IV.

DISTRICTS DESCRIBED IN DETAIL.

The .following pages contain descriptions of some selected areas in Manchester and Salford. In each case, the description is based on the results of a house-to-house enquiry carried out during 1902 and carefully checked. The areas were chosen as the result of a general survey made in 1901 when information, in general terms, as to the conditions prevailing in different parts of the towns, was obtained from many clergymen, ministers, medical men, and others, whose duties brought them much in contact with the people. We are glad to say that in a number of cases, through the action of the sanitary authorities, the areas have since been improved or are undergoing improvement, and the conditions now are not as described. But our areas were merely examples, and serve to show the citizens of our towns under what condition some of their neighbours live. For, although improvements have been effected in some of the areas examined, it would not be difficult to enumerate others in which the conditions are still equally bad. Since the detailed examination was completed we have submitted our descriptive summaries to the scrutiny of ministers of religion and others working in the districts.

Following the summaries of the conditions in each district, we have given in tabular form a series of extracts from the visitors' note-books. These have been chosen carefully to illustrate the good as well as the bad revealed by a systematic investigation. It will be seen by the reader that in nearly every district there are houses in good repair, well kept by the tenants, and, although not up to first-class sanitary requirements, more or less wholesome dwellings if neighbouring insanitary dwellings were removed. There are many houses, in the districts described and in other parts of Manchester and Salford, which are just beginning, from lack of repair or from careless treatment by the tenants, to approach the line which separates them from slum property. To these houses public attention ought to be directed as much as, if not more than, to existing slums.

We have not indicated the exact location of the areas to avoid causing inconvenience to individual tenants. In the appendix, the Schedule used by the investigators is reprinted.

DISTRICT No. 1 IN ANCOATS.

General. The district examined covers an area of 12·67 acres, being roughly 307 yards across and 200 yards deep. It forms a rough parallelogram, the boundaries being streets of fair width. The district is almost entirely residential though factories and works are quite near. It contains nearly 600 dwellings, varying in size from six to two rooms. Houses of the latter type are back-to-back and are gradually tending to disappear under pressure from the Sanitary Committee of the Corporation. The streets are narrow with few exceptions, and there are several cul-de-sacs and courts. There is no open space in the district, though the remains of a croft exist at the north-east corner of the district. This is used as a playground by the children and youths of the neighbourhood, but after wet weather is in a filthy state.

The inhabitants are poor, and none of them are far removed from actual want. In many cases the visitor found that the family was in real distress for lack of means. " Labourer " is the usual return given as the occupation of the head of the household, though carter, railway worker, packer, and other similar occupations occur. Very few skilled workers were found in the district, and a large proportion of those found were out of work. The investigators noted that they were often old men, occasionally they were invalids, and in a few cases there was evidence that they were intemperate. In a good many instances the head of the household was a widow earning money by charing or washing. The younger members of the families seem to earn good wages in comparison with their seniors, boys being employed in mills or becoming labourers at an early age; girls going to mills or serving in shops.

Twelve licensed houses are to be found in the district and there are many more immediately outside. This may be stated in other words as one licence to every 40 houses. A church is just outside the area on the south side, and at the north-east corner there is another church with a large People's Institute and schools in connection with it.

The most marked feature of the district on walking through it is its dulness. There is a complete absence of trees, and there is seemingly little attempt to grow plants or to otherwise brighten the homes. This is the more marked since evidences of effort in this direction are to be seen in the wider streets before one enters the district, and even in the wider of the streets crossing the district itself.

Population, overcrowding and health of area. The statistics given by the Medical Officer of Health, in his latest report, show the average density of population for Ancoats as 113 persons to the acre. This statement, of course, applies to the 400 acres included in Ancoats, much space being occupied by railways, canals, and factories. In the small district under discussion, the area of which is 12·67 acres, there are very nearly 47 houses to the acre. From the figures obtained by house-to-house visitation, the average household consists of just over four persons, the actual figure being 4·33. This gives a population density of 203 (202·64) persons to the acre. The ill effects of overcrowding on area are discussed in another place (p. 29). It may suffice here to compare this density with the *average* density of Manchester, which is 42 persons to the acre.

Though a high death-rate and frequent cases of illness are perhaps to be looked for in some parts of Ancoats owing to the large proportion of people earning low wages, and therefore poorly nourished, and to the large proportion who have not the knowledge which would enable them to spend their wages to the greatest advantage, yet some share of the blame for the high mortality must be thrown on the close packing of dwellings on the land, and also on the poor character of many of these dwellings.

Another evidence of untoward conditions in Ancoats is to be found in the report of the Medical Officer of Health, which shows that for the year 1901, in Ancoats, 234 out of every 1,000 children born died before attaining the age of one year.*

Overcrowding in the individual houses is apparently not very common. It has to be remembered that this is now an offence if persisted in, and in any case may lead to inconvenience if the sanitary authorities take action, and that consequently some pains are taken to prevent the discovery of its existence. On the whole, however, we are satisfied that in this district at any rate, overcrowding by the census standard, i.e., more than two people to a room, is relatively uncommon. In several cases bad overcrowding even by this lax standard has been reported, but in these cases there have usually been large families of young children. But here again attention must be drawn to the fact that in a two-roomed house, the whole family sleeps in one bedroom, and that in a three-roomed house with six inhabitants (which by the census standard is not overcrowded) overcrowding will almost certainly take place every night.

It has been noted that the rooms of the houses in this district are small and a little reflection at once convinces one that healthy life in these houses is hardly possible. In a fairly typical street of the district the size of one of the bedrooms is 10 feet by 10 feet by 8 feet 3 inches which cubed is 825 cubic feet. For healthy life some 800 cubic feet of *fresh* air is required every hour by an adult man, and a little less by a woman. In such a room as this it may be taken for granted that there is not 800 cubic feet of air space, since furniture, though often scanty, occupies some space. Yet rarely does one find a room of this kind used as a sleeping place for one person only, and examples are not lacking of three and four (in one case six) people occupying such a room at night. And the requirements are that the air shall be fresh. In these houses partly for warmth, partly from ignorance, windows are

---

* As shown on the table given on p. 42, the rate of mortality for children under one year dropped in 1902 to 178 per 1,000 births.

not regularly opened, and they are very rarely kept open
at night, so for hours each night the occupants breathe and
re-breathe polluted and poisonous air.

A word may be said here as to the causes of this overcrowding. Rents in the district are going up, especially for
the smaller houses. With the low earnings, often uncertain,
of those who live in the neighbourhood there goes a natural
desire to keep the fixed charges on the week's income as low
as possible. Hence a tenant, even though he dislikes the house,
will stay, lest he should find it impossible to get an equally
cheap house elsewhere. Another factor, slight as yet, is said
to be at work keeping some of the dwellers in the district still
in their overcrowded houses. It is that agents and landlords
have a natural prejudice against tenants from a neighbourhood
which has a bad name, and thus a tenant may be prevented
from finding a better house. How far this statement is true
we do not know.

The houses. There are not many one-roomed dwellings in
this district. By far the larger number are two-roomed and
four-roomed houses. Many of the former are back-to-back
dwellings; the latter are of the familiar " two up, two down "
type. A good many three-roomed houses are to be found, most
of them with a small scullery. In the case of other than back-
to-back houses, the most frequent ground of complaint is that
the houses are kept in poor repair. In many cases walls and
ceilings are falling; often, too, the houses are damp owing to
neglect of roof repairs. There is no doubt that in some cases
the internal disrepair of the house is due primarily to the
carelessness of the tenants, but in other cases the age of the
house should be sufficient ground for careful and systematic
repairing. It has been said more than once by tenants—we
do not know with how much truth—that the landlord will not
execute repairs because the property is to be condemned. The
pity is that the condemnation is not made effective.

Rents show a considerable range. For a two-roomed house
in one street the same rent is asked as for a four-roomed house
in a neighbouring street. The cost of a two-roomed house is
from 2s. 9d. to 4s. 6d. weekly, the average rental being 3s. 5d.
Three rooms are rented at from 2s. 9d. to 5s. 9d. weekly; the

average rent being just under 4s. 3d. per week. A four-roomed house lets at from 3s. 3d. to 7s., the average being almost 4s. 10d. One room with a scullery rents at 3s. 2d., without a scullery at 2s. 6d. Five-roomed houses let at rents varying from 5s. 6d. to 6s. 6d. Of the houses examined, ·44·5 per cent. had four rooms, 34·8 per cent. two rooms, 15·7 per cent. three rooms, 3 per cent. five rooms, and 2 per cent. one room.

DISTRICT No. 2 IN St. JOHN'S WARD.

The investigation in this district has covered only a small area, but the results are important. The area described below abuts on a street occupied for the most part by professional men's chambers and on one of the most important business thoroughfares in the city.

Special attention has been given to a series of courts leading off a narrow back street. Three of these courts are culs-de-sac. The other two, which lie on the opposite side of the street, have narrow exits into the street beyond.

The three cul-de-sac courts to the north contain 25 dwelling-houses, a shop, and a lodging-house. Each court is 21 yards long; one is 10½ feet, the other two are 17½ feet wide. The width of the street on which they open is 24 feet. The courts are flagged, with a gutter in the centre, but the fall is poor and the water often stands.

The houses are all old, probably built early last century, three storeys high and back-to-back. The average population at the time of investigation was 4·75 persons to a house. Two of the houses were to let and on a more recent visit, it was found that another house was to let. The tenants chiefly belong to the unskilled labour class.

The rent of each house is 4s. 3d. per week, except for the corner houses facing the street, which let at 4s. 6d. Each house covers an area of 12 feet 6 inches by 15 feet. Each contains a living room measuring 11 feet 9 inches by 20 feet 6 inches by 8 feet 4 inches, a bedroom of the same size and another bedroom 14 feet 5 inches by 10 feet 6 inches by 7 feet 4 inches. There are no pantries and no provision for the

	Head of House, Occupation, and Ear	NOTES AND REMARKS
1	Striker, 20	Back-to-back house, end of row. Entry beside it. Ceilings and walls very damp and cracked.
8	Moulder, 4	Smells from privy and drains. Tenant said sanitary authorities were putting pressure on landlord to repair house.
13	Labourer,	Daughter of tenant and four children temporary residents.
18	Labourer,	House dark, owing to small windows. Closet very old and tumble-down. One room is not used.
26	Market ma	Walls damp. Yard shared by two houses.
29	Carter, 22/	
2	Labourer,	
4	Baker, 26/	
8	Wife of sol	Husband at Gibraltar. Wife allowed 1s. 11d. per day. Six sleepers in bedroom of 893 cub. ft.
9	Widow, se	House very dirty, and damp from continuous washing going on in house. Water standing in yard.
5	Labourer,	Extra ½d. on rent is charged for cleaning closets weekly.
2	Glass-mou	Back-to-back house. Four closets for eight houses. Tenants say they prefer two-roomed house, as there is less house-work
		Extra bedroom over closets. Closets very dirty. Ashes spilt all over seats

washing of clothes. Each house has an oven, and also a water-tap and sink in a cupboard.

The houses are kept in very fair repair and most of the tenants appear to be cleanly. The rooms are well ventilated, each having a fireplace and an openable window and they are dry. The windows are not large, and partly owing to this, partly owing to the neighbouring buildings, the rooms are dark. The closets are pail closets placed in the court, one being provided for every three houses. One set are kept locked, but the others are open. Two ashpits are provided for every five houses.

Of fourteen families questioned, no fewer than nine said they could live away from the district if they could have a cheap tram service before 6 a.m. Most of them added that they were attached to the district by old associations and would be reluctant to move.

The courts on the south side of the street also contain old houses, which are kept in poor repair by the landlord and are also neglected by the tenants. Many of the floors and stair-cases were found in such bad repair that they were described by the investigator as dangerous. Rents vary from 2s. 6d. to 4s.

Seventeen houses have three rooms, one has two rooms, two have four rooms, and one has six rooms. The size of the rooms varies from 10 feet 6 inches by 10 feet 6 inches to 16 feet by 10 feet 8 inches; the average floor area is about 11 feet square. The houses are all back-to-back. The four and six-roomed houses mentioned have two rooms on a floor; the back one receiving its light from the front room through a window in the partition wall. The larger court is 19½ feet wide at one end, but only 12 feet wide at the other. Of two houses it is reported that the top rooms are closed up, as the roof leaks beyond possibility of repair. One house has a small scullery. Several houses have cellars, though these are not always in use. One locked cellar contained refuse from which un-pleasant odours reached the room above through gaps in the floor.

There is only one water-tap for all the houses in the two courts and this is apparently used by 26 families. It is placed in the larger court beside the closets and in frosty weather is frequently out of order. The sanitary conveniences are pail closets, placed in the court and facing the house doors. They are described as being in a very unwholesome condition, only two out of five being fit to use. The doors have neither lock nor other fastening. A tenant explained that keys had at one time been provided, but they got lost and the locks were then broken off. People from the next street also use the closets.*

DISTRICT No. 3 IN ST. MICHAEL's WARD.

The part of this district investigated has been frequently cited by writers dealing with housing conditions in Manchester, as an example of what a district ought not to be. It has been included in this investigation as an illustration of a process which may take place in other districts of Manchester. Several streets in the district are lined by houses of considerable age and evidently built for moderately well-to-do families. As the neighbourhood became less desirable, these families have moved to other parts, and the houses have been occupied by poorer families and finally have become lodging-houses. Two types of lodging-houses occur, the common lodging-house, which for our present purpose is left out of account, and, the house " let in furnished lodgings," which is used as a more or less permanent home. In the latter type, the rooms are sparingly furnished and a tenant, who sometimes resides in the house but often does not, sublets the rooms, singly or two together, to separate families. The houses thus become of the " tenement " type (see p. 34). Modern hygiene protests against a *one-roomed* house, even when provided with modern sanitary appliances. This type of lodging-house, of which examples

---

* NOTE.—Since this description was written, great changes have been made in the area. The back-to-back houses have been converted into through houses and proper sanitary accommodation provided. We are, however, informed that the state of these houses had been much as we describe it for many years.

Dis

To face page 60.

	Head of Household, Occupation, and Earnings Standard?	NOTES AND REMARKS
1	Carter, 20/-	Back-to-back house. Closet supposed to be for three houses. In reality one closet is used by all families in court. A water tap in the centre is used by all families in this court and next, in all about 26.
4	Electrician's labou	Floor of top room so weak as to be dangerous. Family lives and sleeps in one room. (see note above).
5	Labourer, 17/-	Ceilings and wall in bad repair. Bad smells from court.
8	Boatman	Back-to-back house like others in court. Each floor has two rooms, the back one cut off from front room and receiving light by window in the partition. Top floor closed because roof leaks. Man and wife lodge in first floor rooms ; tenants on ground floor rooms.
3	Widow, washerwoman, 5/-	House shares narrow yard in which are two closets for three houses.
6	Labourer	Closets (see next note) so bad that tenants use closet belonging to a friend in a neighbouring street.
10	Docker	Five pail closets serve 19 houses. Closets in filthy state, used by strangers from street. Water supply from next court (see note above).
15	Washerwoman	Closet common to other houses in Court, only 3yds. from house door.
14	Labourer	
16	Iceman	Closets in this case are locked.
21	Shopkeeper (wido	Closet used is one of those in court noted above. This house has a cellar in which is water tap.
26	Salesm	Two closets in —— Place serve five houses, of which this is one.
2	Packing case mak	Court on which house opens is 5½yds. wide. House back-to-back. Overcrowded.
4	Newspaper agent	
5	Drainer	Tenant has lived in country and wants to get back there, but cannot under existing circumstances

are found in Angel Meadow, sometimes does not even have the sanitary provision, which, according to modern ideas, would be considered adequate if the house were occupied only by one family.

The district is a poor one. More than the usual difficulty has been experienced in getting information as to the occupations of the inhabitants. Information was obtained from 102 households. Of these the heads of the household—

In 47 cases said they were labourers.
  ,, 15   ,,   ,,   porters (market and others).
  ,, 13   ,,   ,,   hawkers.
  ,, 2   ,,   ,,   flower dealers.
  ,, 2   ,,   ,,   brokers.
  ,, 7   ,,   ,,   carters.
  ,, 5   ,,   ,,   shoemakers.

In 11 cases the head of the household was a widow with no defined occupation, an income being derived from casual employment, from children's labour, or from parish relief.

In all 11 streets and four courts, containing 273 houses, have been examined. Owing to clearances in connection with railway extensions at one corner of the district, and as a result of interference by the City Council in other parts, a number of houses have been closed and are in process of demolition. It is understood that other houses in the district are also scheduled and will be closed.

From a sanitary point of view the district is in a backward state. Most of the houses are old; in many instances they are in want of structural repair, and they are frequently damp. Where there are yards they are small and gloomy, and used as receptacles for refuse. The water supply is deficient; rarely does a house possess a water-tap for its own exclusive use. The figures given in this table give some idea of the state of affairs, though only a personal inspection of the streets and of the taps can give a true picture.

Houses Sharing One Water-Tap.

In A Street	...	... ...	...	...	...	40 houses.
„ B „	...	... ...	...	...	...	22	„
„ C „	...	... ...	...	...	...	20	,.
„ D „	...	... ...	...	...	...	12	„
„ E „	...	... ...	...	...	...	10	„
„ F „	...	... ...	...	...	...	9	„
„ G „	...	... ...	...	...	..	7	„
„ H „	...	... ...	...	...	...	6	„
., I „	...	.. ...	...	...	...	6	.,
„ K „	...	... ...	...	...	...	5	„

With the exception of 20 houses, each of which has a w.c., the conveniences are pail closets. In several streets the closets are placed, as is usual with back-to-back houses, in a group, and are entered directly from the street. Used as they are by members of more than one household, and by casual visitors from the street, the sense of the responsibility for keeping the closets clean and wholesome seems to have departed from the district. The doors stand open and frequently display a reeking, filthy, and sickening accumulation which reflects not only on the dwellers in the district, but on the citizens at large who allow such things to exist. The photographs reproduced fail to indicate adequately the conditions which prevail.

Twenty-three cases were found of *one-roomed* dwellings. In all cases the room was let as a furnished lodging on the system which seems characteristic of the neighbourhood. The rents charged per furnished room vary from 4s. to 5s. 10d. and the average is nearly 5s. 2d. per week. When it is remembered that the sanitary condition of many of these houses is deplorable and that the furnishing is nominal, consisting usually of a bed, with some sort of table, and, it may be, a chair or two—often of a very makeshift kind—the rents charged do not seem too low. On the other hand, it must be said that there is evidence that tenants frequently leave without paying rent.

The rents of unfurnished two-roomed houses vary from 2s. 6d. to 4s. 3d. per week; if there is a scullery from 3s. 6d.

	Head of Household, pation, and Earnings	NOTES AND REMARKS
11	Uncertain	House let in lodgings, three families having a room each. House very dirty and neglected. Walls and ceilings damp and cracked.
4	Market porter, 1	Attic bedroom damp; rain comes in through ceiling.
12 A B	Labourer, 18/– Hawker, 26/–	House let as " furnished " lodgings.
9	Toy maker, 28/–	Industry carried on at home.
27	Labourer, 22/–	Yard is shared by three houses.
29	Dyer, pays wife	Yard as above. House very damp. Two front rooms in very bad repair.
52	Labourer, 19/–	House neglected both by landlord and tenant.
8	Cutler, out of wo Railway laboure 19/–	Two families in house, each occupy two rooms.
44	Slipper maker, 2	Family of immigrant aliens.
9	Carter, 28/–	This house is let " furnished."
15	Labourer, out of	Back-to-back house. Five sleepers in bedroom of 990 cub. ft. Closets in shocking state.

to 4s. 6d. per week. The average rent for two rooms is about 3s. 4d.; for two rooms and scullery 3s. 9d. But two-roomed houses are also let "furnished" at rentals varying from 4s. 8d. to 7s.; the average rental being 5s. 10d.

For three unfurnished rooms, we found that a rent varying from 3s. 3d. to 5s. 10d. was asked; the average rent being 4s. 2½d. More than half the three-roomed houses visited had sculleries; the rents of these are higher, from 3s. 6d. to 6s., the average being 4s. 8d. Only six of the three-roomed houses visited were let furnished, the rents being from 5s. 3d. to 7s. (two houses at 5s. 11½d.); the average 5s. 9½d.

Four-roomed houses were found to be rented at from 3s. 6d. to 8s. The average rent was about 5s. 6d. per week. The average rent of the houses with sculleries was a trifle lower, about 5s. 5½d., and 11 houses were let furnished at an average rent of 5s. 6d. The four-roomed houses used as common lodging-houses are rented at 11s. 6d. each.

Some 19 five-roomed houses were visited, one-third of them let as furnished lodgings. For houses of five unfurnished rooms rents vary from 6s. to 9s. (the latter rent being exceptionally high), with an average of 6s. 2d. Furnished the average is 6s. 4d.

It will be noticed that the same money commands a considerable range in accommodation, and in the case of four-roomed houses, there is little difference in the cost of an unfurnished and a "furnished" house. The average rents of furnished houses are interesting when compared.

AVERAGE WEEKLY RENTAL.

One Room.	Two Rooms.	Three Rooms.	Four Rooms.	Five Rooms.
5s. 2d.	5s. 10d.	5s. 9½d.	5s. 8d.	6s. 4d.

We would remind readers that the rentals have in nearly all cases been given by the tenants and that our investigation only covered a limited area. But from comparison with information supplied by others, we believe the account we have given in the foregoing pages to be true of the greater part of the residential district contiguous to Smithfield Market.

DISTRICT No. 4 IN ARDWICK.

A small district in Ardwick Ward has been investigated, lying near the L. and N.-W. Railway. Many persons must have noticed the closely packed and gloomy streets seen from the railway just before entering London Road Station from the south. Our purpose has been to get information which would enable those who reach Manchester by train to realise the condition under which people live in these streets.

The area investigated is bounded on three sides by important streets. It contains 31 streets and 476 houses, of which 37 were unoccupied when the visits were made. There are 11 licensed houses in the area, or one to every 43 residences and there are many licensed houses in the streets near the district investigated. Two mills, a brewery, a mission room, and a school are also in the district. There are two open spaces not very far from the district, one of them arranged as a recreation ground.

Most of the houses are old, not a few are worn out. The streets are narrow and dark, and houses are built so close to the railway that they are deprived of light.[1] No fewer than 71 of the houses visited are back-to-back. Many of the dwellers in the district are poor. The occupations followed are similar to those reported from other districts investigated—labourers, carters, warehousemen, platelayers, etc., with a small proportion of skilled workers.

In several cases in this district the tenants complained of smells from the drains. The smells were evident to the visitor but it is not known how far they may be attributed to the drains. The streets—especially the back ones—and the entries are dirty, and are used as receptacles for refuse. Sixty-nine houses have no separate water supply, and share five taps in this manner:—

---

[1] An extensive clearance in view of railway extension has removed the houses referred to, although there are houses to be seen on the other side of the railway which have dark rooms.

In Ardwick. A narrow passage leads to a court behind the front row of houses.

In Ardwick. Interior of the court seen in picture above. Ten houses to one water-tap.

To face p. 64.

	Head of Household, Occupation, and Earnings Stated	NOTES AND REMARKS
12	Driller, 24/-	Smells from closet. House old and damp. Five sleep in one bedroom, four in another. Tap in yard.
25	Shaper, 29/-	House very damp.
26	Foundryman, 30/-	Rooms very small. Bedroom for two adults has cubic content of 512ft. Typical of other houses in street.
33	Moulder, 20/-	House very dirty.
35	Carter, 22/-	Lodgers pay 2s. weekly for living room. Very dirty house.
6	Carter, 26/-	House has usable cellar. Three bedrooms.
7	—	
12	Painter, 35/-	House has cellar, in which is copper for clothes washing.
2	Washerwoman, 8/ (see note)	Husband of tenant in South Africa; sends wife 2s. 6d. weekly. Her mother lodges with her, pays 3s. Smells from closet. Rooms low and dark.
6	Watchman, 20/-	House old and damp. Said to be condemned.
12	—	Back-to-back house. Tap in entry. Smells from drains (?) and closets. House dirty.
1	Washerwoman, 9/	Back-to-back house.
3	Widow, washes	Back-to-back house. Smells from drains (?) Three adults sleep in one bedroom (825 cub. ft.).

20 houses	use	1 tap.
16	,,	,,
15	,,	,,
10	,,	,,
8	,,	,,
69 ·		5 taps.

Sanitary conveniences are more numerous than in some other districts examined, and on the whole are better kept. There are 31 water closets; 25 houses have one each, while other 12 houses have one w.c. between two houses. In 287 cases, the house has a separate pail closet; the remaining houses share pail closets; five, four, three or two houses using one.

The houses visited were two, three, four, or five-roomed. Rents for two-roomed houses vary from 2s. 6d. to 3s. 9d.; the average rent being about 3s. 1d. Rents of three-roomed houses, which in most cases have a scullery, vary from 3s. to 5s.; average rent 4s. 1d. Four-roomed houses have rents from 3s. 6d. to 6s.; with an average of 4s. 7½d. Two four-roomed houses used as shops pay rents of 7s. 11d. and 12s. Five-roomed houses are rented at from 4s. 3d. to 6s.; the average rent being 5s. 6½d. More than half of the houses examined have four rooms.

There were 71 back-to-back houses among those visited. Some houses which were back-to-back have been made " through " houses. The visitors' reports for street after street remark that the houses are damp and that bad smells prevail. In very many instances the visitor notes that the house is dirty and out of repair.

DISTRICT No. 5 IN HULME.

The area investigated in Hulme is a small one of seven streets, comprising 143 houses. The area adjoins one which has received much attention from the authorities because of the insanitary property in it, and in the streets examined there are a number of houses which have been altered to " through " from back-to-back houses. Back-to-back houses, however, still remain in the area.

There are five licensed houses in the area, and others just outside.

The houses contain two, three or four rooms, and in one case five rooms. The two-roomed houses are in the streets in which the houses are back-to-back. In very few cases is there a scullery and only three houses had cellars.

Sixteen of the houses, in very bad repair, were said to be condemned. In another street eight houses are said to be much in want of repair, the walls and ceilings being cracked and falling, and the houses damp. Evil smells are a cause of complaint. The smells are due to neighbouring manufactories.

As in other districts where there are many back-to-back houses, the supply of water and of sanitary conveniences is most inadequate. To 30 dwellings there is only one tap, which the investigator notes is always leaking. Another 11 houses share one tap. In another street 10 houses have only one tap, placed in a narrow entry between them. Seven other houses have one tap.

Thirty-two houses have water closets; one closet to two houses. Most of the houses have each a pail closet. But in several streets the closet accommodation varies from one closet for *four* houses to one closet for *eight* houses. The closets are not well kept and are offensive.

The inhabitants are poor, labourers for the most part, with, according to their statements, low earnings.

The rents charged in the district are: For a two-roomed house, from 3s. 3d. to 4s. 6d., the average for the houses visited being just over 4s. per week; for a three-roomed house, from 3s. 3d. to 4s., the average rent being about 3s. 7d.; for a three-roomed house, with a scullery, from 4s. 3d. to 5s. 3d., the average being 4s. 6½d.; and for a four-roomed house, from 3s. 9d. to 6s., the average rent being 4s. 8½d. per week. One house of five rooms and a scullery was let at 6s. 4d. per week. The curious fact that three-roomed houses are let at lower rents than two-roomed houses is accounted for in this case by the inclusion of a considerable number of old houses in bad repair among the three-roomed houses.

	Head of Household, Occupation, and Earnings Stated	NOTES AND REMARKS
2	French polisher, 22/-	Converted back-to-back house. Yard shared with another house.
9	Labourer, 19/6	Rooms very small and overcrowded bedrooms House in bad repair.
10	Flagger, 20/-	Five sleepers in one room.
14	Labourer, 19/-	
23	Carter, 22/-	House in poor repair. Bad smells from closet.
7	Charwoman, 10/- to 12/-	House one in a row of back-to-back houses which have been reconstructed to give yards.
3	Packer, out of work	Exceptionally clean and respectable family.
15	Factory hand, 17/-	
4	Labourer, 18/-	Tenants untidy ; given to drink.
6	Labourer, 14/-	This and neighbouring houses are condemned. Tenants are living free rent. Smells from rubber factory apparent.
7	Laundrywoman	Back-to-back house. Eight closets are placed together in centre of block, about one closet for three houses. Behind closets is a wash house with a copper, but the tenants say it is seldom used.
11	— ?	

In Chorlton-on-Medlock. Back-to-back houses being made "through" houses, alternate houses coming down.

In Chorlton-on-Medlock. Old houses facing dead wall; one closet for six houses.

To face p. 67.

DISTRICT No. 6 IN CHORLTON-UPON-MEDLOCK.

The area investigated in this district is irregular in outline, and really consists of several small contiguous areas. The district contains many old houses, but the steady encroachment of the business part of the town is constantly causing their disappearance. In no part of the town have we found worse conditions prevailing among the homes of the people. In many streets the houses are small, overshadowed by high buildings and walls, in bad repair, and very deficient in conveniences. There are several groups of back-to-back dwellings.[1]

There are no shops or public-houses in the streets covered by the house-to-house investigation, but in neighbouring streets there are many licensed houses. The tenants in the area seem poorer than in any other district examined, and the houses and their surroundings are dirtier and less cared for than in other parts of the town. Many houses are said to be damp, and of several the investigators report that rain comes in through the roofs. There were frequent complaints made that the houses swarmed with vermin, and that sour, nauseating smells from ashpits and privies were noticeable. The investigators in every case report that the district gives them the impression of hopeless squalor and misery.

The residents in the district depend almost entirely on casual and very irregular work. Of 39 heads of households who stated their occupations, eleven were labourers, seven were charwomen, three were carters, two stonemasons, two hawkers, two warehouse porters; while the following occupations had each one representative:—Watchman, bootmender, dyeworker, property-repairer, iron-driller, leather-dresser, painter, plumber, tailor, blacksmith, box-cutter, waste-worker.

The houses visited contained four, three or two rooms. The two-roomed houses were all back-to-back houses. The rents current were: For a four-roomed house, 4s. 6d. per week; for a

---

[1] We have learned while this report was in the press, that some of the back-to-back houses mentioned are being converted into "through" houses. Opposite, a picture is given of the houses in process of conversion.

f

three-roomed house, from 3s. 9d. to 3s. 6d. per week (only two
houses of three rooms being let at the lower rental); for two-
roomed houses, from 3s. 6d. to 3s. 3d. per week. It will be seen,
on comparison with the figures given for other districts, that the
rents of two-roomed houses are slightly higher, and of three-
and four-roomed houses slightly lower in this district than the
averages of other districts.

DISTRICT No. 7 IN SALFORD.

The area investigated forms a rough triangle. On two sides
it is bounded by works and factories. The third side is formed
by a street of some importance in which many of the houses
are used as small shops by confectioners, greengrocers,
provision dealers, and the like. There are five licensed houses
in the area, two with full licenses, one with a beer " on," and
two with beer " off " licenses. In one of the boundary streets
and facing the area are five licensed houses.

A school and mission room are within the area, and there
is a well-equipped Lads' Club outside. It is a district of mean
streets; the streets themselves narrow and dirty, the houses old,
out of repair, and many occupied by careless and untidy
tenants. In the near neighbourhood the sanitary authorities
have made several clearances, notably of back-to-back houses.
The plot on which these houses stood is at present vacant,
advertised as a building lot. The district would benefit if
steps could be taken to preserve the site as an open space. In
one part of the area, the houses have been carefully repaired
and the backs especially improved. In these cases a patent
ashbin has replaced the old ashpit or barrel which is still to be
seen in neighbouring streets. Smells, which are unpleasant
if not unwholesome, are caused by one or more of the factories
near.

There are 310 houses in the area investigated, and of these
99 are back-to-back. Only in one street of the fifteen in the
area are there cellars to the houses. The cellars on one side
of this street have apparently been formerly occupied as
separate dwellings, but they are now closed. Those on the

	Head of Household, Occupation, and Where in Yard?	NOTES AND REMARKS
1	Labourer, s	Three houses share yard in which are a closet and wash-place. House dirty. Dark owing to nearness of wall.
5	Box cutter, s	Wall behind house darkens living room. Seven sleepers in one room. Houses infested by vermin (mice and bugs).
6	Labourer	Evil smells from closets behind belonging to other houses. House has cellar which is unfit for use.
8	Hawker,	All sleep in one room.
1	Labourer	Back-to-back house. Walls wet and structure in bad repair. Roof leaks. One tap in street apparently serves some 50 houses in this and next street. Six closets and one ash place serve one side of street. Closets in filthy condition.
3	Dyer, 30/	Very damp house. Roof falling in. House dark because of nearness of opposite houses. Six

other side of the street are used for wood-chopping, storing, etc. Many of the houses in the area are said to be damp and to be infested by rats and other vermin. In the back passages between the houses and in the courts pools of stagnant water are standing several days after there has been rain.

Each house has its own water-tap. The majority of the houses have yards and closets. Many of the yards are very untidy, and ashpits and closets are in many cases in a filthy condition. In one street, where clothes are dried after washing day, 12 ashpits are without doors. The street is a wide back street.

In 3 cases 7 houses share 1 closet.
In 2 ,, 5 ,, ,, ,,
In 6 ,, 4 ,, ,, ,,
In 2 ,, 3 ,, ,, ,,
In 9 ,, 2 ,, ,, ,,

In practice the number of houses using one closet must be greater than the figures given above indicate, as several closets are quite unfit for use. In one court there are three closets for 11 houses, but only one of the closets can be used, the others being entirely dilapidated.

The residents in the area are, for the most part, unskilled labourers, though a few describe themselves as mechanics, joiners, and so on. When questioned as to their earnings they, in most cases, put them at less than a pound per week.

The rents are, on an average, for a two-roomed house, 3s. 2¼d., and the same average rent obtains for two rooms with a cellar; for a three-roomed house 4s.; for three rooms and a scullery 4s. 6d.; for a four-roomed house 4s. 9d. In one street there are four-roomed houses with sculleries which let at 4s.

On the folding page details are given of a number of houses.

CHAPTER V.

Town Councils, House Owners, and Tenants.

In the preceding chapters, we have endeavoured to give a picture of existing conditions in typical parts of Manchester and Salford. We may now with advantage consider what are the powers and what are the limitations of our Town Councils and others in dealing with these conditions.

(a) *Town Councils.* Very extensive powers in dealing with unwholesome conditions in the houses of the people are now given to Town Councils. As the local health authority, the Town Council has power to close insanitary houses and, if they cannot be remedied, to have them demolished. Where the general conditions of the property in a neighbourhood are detrimental to the health of the inhabitants, the area may be scheduled and cleared. A wide discretion is left to the local authority as to what conditions are detrimental to health. These conditions may be overcrowding on the land, bad building, bad repair and the like, or a combination of any or all of these.

The Town Council is also entrusted with the supervision of new dwellings erected in the city, and it is its duty to carefully examine the plans, and supervise the work while in progress to ensure that new houses shall be at least sanitary dwellings.

These duties are imposed on Town Councils mainly by legislation of the type of the Public Health Acts. The results of the municipal action, which has been taken under this kind of legislation, are to be found in the lowered death-rates in our towns, and in the relative infrequency of the most dangerous infectious diseases nowadays as compared with 20 or 30 years ago. But although the average expectation of life may be greater and the liability to disease less, it is open to doubt whether the vitality of our town populations has improved during, say, the last 30 years. Evidence goes to show that in physique, vitality, and energy our town populations of to-day compare unfavourably with those of earlier years, although, on the whole, wages are higher and food is cheaper. And to-day the proportion of our people influenced by town conditions of life is far higher than it was 30 years ago.

The duties mentioned are carried out by committees of the Town Councils, in Manchester principally by the Sanitary Committee and the Improvement and Buildings Committee. Other Committees, for example, the Cleansing, Parks, Waterworks, Paving and Sewering Committees, attend to matters closely connected with the public health. The executive work of the Sanitary Committee is done by the Medical Officer of Health, the Sanitary Superintendent, and a staff of inspectors. The sanitary inspectors have districts allotted to them and are expected to keep a close watch for conditions prejudicial to health. The reports are submitted to the Medical Officer of Health, who advises the committee on the steps to be taken. In the event of infectious disease occurring in his district, the sanitary inspector has to see that the instructions of the Medical Officer are carried out. It will be obvious that the efficient performance of those duties is only possible when the inspector has a small district. Regular inspection of *every* house in the district ought to be made and such inspection should be welcomed by the citizens. But the difficulty of efficient inspection must at present be great. In 1903, Manchester had 28 district inspectors at work, with, by the last census returns, 108,957 *inhabited* houses. This gives each inspector an average of 3,891 houses to supervise, a number, we believe, to be too large for one man. An increase in the number of inspectors is urgently needed. A number of other inspectors are engaged on special work.[1]

In Salford the Health Committee of the Council performs functions similar to those of the Sanitary Committee of Manchester. The executive officials are, as in Manchester, the Medical Officer and the sanitary inspectors. Here, too, a large increase in the inspecting staff is desirable, though the work of remedying existing bad conditions is in Salford being very actively carried out. The 1901 census records 44,001 inhabited houses in Salford. In 1903, the inspecting staff consisted of

[1] The visitors of the Ladies' Public Health Society help in the work of Sanitary inspection both in Manchester and Salford.

a chief and an assistant inspector, six district inspectors and a lady inspector, with others engaged in special work. If the district inspectors only have areas assigned to them, each of them has, on an average, 7,337 houses.

The work done by the existing staffs, both in City and Borough, deserves hearty approval from the citizens. We feel that this can best be given by an expression of public opinion in favour of more frequent and more detailed inspection and, as we have pointed out, this will necessarily mean an increase in the numbers of the staff.

Legislation during the last quarter of the nineteenth century, and especially during the last decade, has extended the power of Town Councils far beyond the mere suppression of conditions injurious to health. Parliament has recognised that action in this direction almost certainly involves dishousing part of the population, and that a part for which suitable accommodation seems more and more difficult to find, and also that a deficiency in the supply of wholesome houses is responsible for overcrowding and other insanitary conditions. It has, therefore, given municipalities power to erect houses for the working classes. In the earlier acts this was confined to the power of rebuilding on sites previously occupied by insanitary dwellings, but, under the Housing of the Working Classes Acts, 1890 and 1900, this power has been widened so that now the local authority may acquire land for house building purposes either within or without the town boundaries. An account of the building operations carried on by the Town Councils of Manchester and Salford and of other towns will be found in the succeeding chapter.

(b) *Tenants.* It would be out of place here to discuss at length the rights of tenants. Briefly the tenant is entitled to insist that the dwelling for which he pays rent shall be sanitary, and, as a ratepayer, he is entitled to expect good surroundings to his dwelling. That many people in our towns live in dwellings which are not sanitary has been amply demonstrated. In some of these cases the tenants hesitate to complain for fear that they may be turned out, or that, if any improvement is effected, the rent may be raised, which in many instances would mean ejection. The action of our local authorities, too, is to some extent limited by similar considerations. To make large clearances in some parts of the city is desirable, but, until provision has been made elsewhere for those who will be dishoused, the authorities dare not take action lest matters become worse in other districts. The most insanitary areas are those occupied by the poorest classes, who are often the least intelligent and most careless part of the population. They cannot be expected to take the initiative in remedying matters, and the community, on its own behalf as much as on their behalf, must see that they are given the external conditions of healthy life. We have already described the powers in this direction possessed by our Town Councils. Much good use of these powers has been made in recent years. We think that the half-hearted support given to the Town Councils by the ratepayers is one of the chief obstacles to the fuller use of these powers.

(c) *Owners.* Just as tenants are entitled to decent dwellings so the owners of houses are entitled to reasonably careful treatment of their property. There is no doubt that there are many cases in which the insanitary and unwholesome state of a house is due primarily to the carelessness or even to the wanton destructiveness of the occupier. It is necessary to insist on this, as frequently the whole blame is thrown on the owner. But while it is difficult for the tenant in many cases to obtain a remedy owing to his weakness, the owner, by his relative strength, should find it easy to protect himself. It is true that popular feeling tends to side more readily with the tenant than with the owner, but we feel sure that a consistent policy among the owners of house property in refusing as tenants those who misuse their dwellings either by overcrowding or by lack of cleanliness, or by actual injury to the structure, would meet with the cordial approval of all interested in bettering housing conditions. From an economic standpoint the position of the landlord would be improved by such action since there would be less likelihood of interference by the health authorities, less need for expenditure on upkeep, and greater certainty of a return from the tenants. The co-operation of the Property Owners' Association and similar bodies on such lines would be a welcome aid towards the improvement of the healthiness of the district.

It may be incidentally noted that combined action on these lines by property owners would ultimately throw on the community the necessity of making provision for those rejected. The scheme of Mr. John Mann (of Glasgow), which has the approval of Professor Smart, deserves consideration. The suggestion, put briefly, is that the Town Council should erect dwellings of the simplest possible kind, substantial in structure, with indestructible fixtures, and let at rents which would simply cover the cost. The residents in these dwellings would be under close supervision of a quasi-police sort. Here the rejected ones would readily be accepted. They would find sanitary conditions and would be disciplined into better ways. The author of the scheme claims that, even if it did not pay its way, the community would save by the improvement in health, and the reduction in crime brought about by the segregation of these undesirables. Moral influences could, of course, be brought to bear on them more readily than under the present system, where they are spread over considerable areas. If the scheme were carried out, it would practically mean the provision of furnished or semi-furnished lodgings for families similar to those already provided by the Town Councils for men in their model lodging-houses.*

---

[1] For fuller details, see "The Housing Problem and the Municipality," by Prof. Wm. Smart, 1902, 1d. Glasgow : Adshead and Son, Union Street.

CHAPTER VI.

THE PROVISION OF WHOLESOME HOUSES.

We have in a previous chapter described some of the evil conditions existing in Manchester and Salford. Similar conditions exist or have existed in many other cities in Great Britain and on the continent, and it is of interest to Manchester citizens to know what has been done elsewhere to cope with these evils. In this chapter we propose to give some account of what has been accomplished by private individuals and companies and by Town Councils.

(a) *Private Effort.* In dealing with bad housing conditions, it is obviously best to take steps to prevent the further deterioration of property and, if possible, to make bad property habitable. Work of this kind has been carried on by Miss Octavia Hill and her friends in London and by other organisations throughout the country. Old property has been purchased and carefully repaired and every effort made to keep it in good repair. Miss Hill introduced the system of having lady rent-collectors, who establish friendly relations with the tenants and represent the landlord. Educative influences can thus be brought to bear on those tenants who by their carelessness and ignorance do harm to the houses in which they reside. The system is essentially one of personal management and responsibility. In Miss Hill's experiments there has been a reasonable return on the capital invested.

In Leeds, largely owing to the efforts of Mr. Edmund Wilson, a limited liability Company has for many years successfully carried on work of a similar kind. It has acquired blocks of property in the more crowded parts of the town, and, by judicious weeding of the worst houses, and careful management of the others, has saved to the town as decent dwellings many houses which otherwise would have been slum property. An interesting account of the work from the pen of Mr. Wilson is to be found in the "Journal of the Society of Arts" for 9th February, 1900.

In other towns, various organisations have undertaken rent collecting on Miss Hill's lines. They collect rents regularly on the understanding that the landlords will carry out such repairs as they consider desirable, and at the same time, by their personal influence brought to bear on the tenants, they help to raise the individuals as well as their surroundings. Work. of this kind is done by some of the ladies of the Kyrle Society in the poorer parts of Glasgow and by the Social Union in Edinburgh. The latter organisation was recently asked by the Edinburgh Town Council to "factor" (*i.e.*, act as agents for) some new blocks of dwellings it had erected.

The value of work of this kind lies in saving for the community a number of houses, which, if treated as so much of the property in the poorer parts of our towns is treated, would soon become uninhabitable and still further increase the difficulties in the way of providing wholesome surroundings for the people.

In London and elsewhere, many companies have been formed to carry out schemes for the better housing of the people. In many cases such companies are limited by their articles of association to a relatively low dividend, say four per cent. Should a surplus be available, it is variously applied to the improvement of the properties, to extending the scheme, to providing facilities for recreation for the tenants, or sometimes in giving a bonus, equivalent to a discount on the rental, to those tenants who have paid regularly. Such companies attract the capital of those who are content with a small return and who have a sense of responsibility respecting the use made of their capital.

Although most companies of this kind have built the dwellings they own, several of them have bought old properties which they have remodelled and made wholesome. In every case attempts have been made to provide dwellings in accord with modern sanitary requirements. It may be noted in passing that the Glasgow Working Men's Dwellings Company Limited, which has both reconstructed property and newly built dwellings, finds the old property the more remunerative.

Mention must also be made of philanthropic organisations

like the Peabody Trust,which have done much to provide good houses, albeit in block dwellings, for some of the working classes. As the earnings of the capital invested accumulate, a fund is formed which will be used in building more houses. The houses are let at rents which an ordinary business undertaking would charge.

The work of such companies and organisations has shown that it is possible, provided the investor is satisfied with a small return on his capital, to give the tenant as much (or more) accommodation as he would get in less satisfactory property for the same money. A large extension of enterprise of this type would doubtless do much to reduce or remove the housing difficulties of the present time. But there is no sign of a move in this direction, probably because, while the return offered is not sufficiently attractive to the ordinary investor, those who would invest capital in such schemes get little encouragement from the municipality. Persons who would take part in such schemes from a desire to benefit the people must wish to have some assurance respecting the surroundings of their property which cannot be obtained with our hap-hazard methods of town extension.

Although the reconstruction and adaptation of old property has in most cases been confined to block dwellings, which are not found in our district, a similar method might be applied with a reasonable hope of success to some of the large houses in parts of Chorlton-on-Medlock and elsewhere. Many large houses in good condition are there standing empty. The rents wanted for them in their present form are too high for working class families, but, if each house were adapted, as it might be, for two families, we believe that they could be let at rents which would be remunerative. Such reconstructed houses would be very similar to the cottage flats which have been found successful in other towns.

Another way in which the housing problem may be made less acute is by employers of labour arranging to house the families of their workers. In recent years there have been many schemes of this kind carried out, both in this country and elsewhere. Where a good plan is adopted and care is taken to see that the houses are well built and that the surroundings are good, there is much to be said in favour of such a scheme. On the other side, there is always the objection that the worker has little independence when he occupies a house owned by the employer. No work, no home! is said to be a current saying among agricultural labourers in England, and other workers are inclined to look askance at any scheme which might conceivably put them in such a position.

The provision of houses for the workers at Saltaire and at Aintree and by several large collieries might be cited as examples of this method of dealing with the question. But it may be well to take perhaps the best known among recent English schemes, that of Messrs. Lever Brothers, Limited, at Port Sunlight. This firm has housed a large number of its workpeople in a village close to their works. The enterprise is frankly unremunerative. The income from rents only covers the cost of maintenance and repairs and does not yield a dividend on the capital invested. The head of the firm describes the scheme as " prosperity sharing "—the best means he can find of sharing profits with his workpeople—and he has recently stated that the firm gets a return in the better health and consequent increased efficiency of the workers. The value of the scheme to those who are interested in the general question of housing lies in the fact that at Port Sunlight the housing conditions are almost ideal. The houses are well built and well planned. A large well-lighted living room with a smaller back kitchen or scullery is provided on the ground floor and there are three bedrooms upstairs. A bath-room has been provided in nearly every house. In every case there is a small garden-patch in front of the house, and at the back there is a good yard with the necessary offices. In different parts of the village there are allotments which are let at nominal rents. Besides the allotments there are numerous open spaces, the roads are wide and well planted with trees, and recreation grounds are provided where tennis, bowls, cricket and football may be played. In this way the surroundings of the houses are made pleasant, and the cheerfulness of the village is in-

LEVER BROS. LTD., PORT SUNLIGHT, CHESHIRE.
THE "SUNLIGHT" PLAN.

FRONT ELEVATION.

GROUND PLAN.

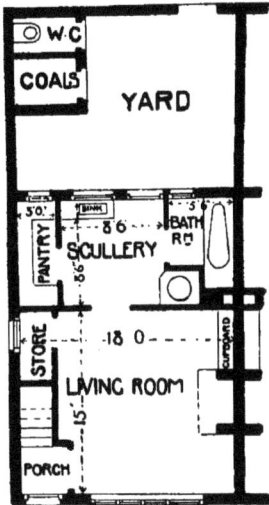

1ST FLOOR PLAN.

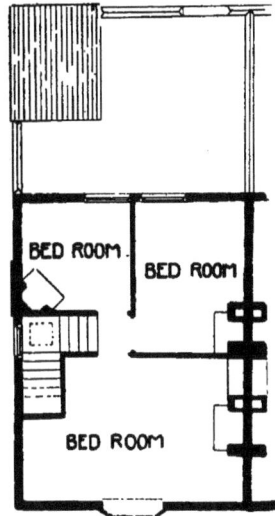

To face p. 78.

creased by the care which has been taken to secure variety of form and colour in the exteriors of the houses.

The experiment of Messrs. Lever Brothers is of great value, first, to those who sympathise with the aims of the Garden City Association in its proposal to take industries into the country and to establish new towns there on model lines; and, secondly, to all who are concerned with the housing of the people, since the village sets an ideal which is not altogether out of reach.

Similar housing schemes have been developed on a large scale by employers of labour in Germany, France, Switzerland and America. The most important on the Continent is that established by the firm of Krupp at Essen, where dwellings for over 26,000 persons have been provided.

The name of Bourneville will almost certainly occur to most readers at this stage. Bourneville differs from Port Sunlight in that residents are not necessarily in the employment of those who provided the houses. Mr. Cadbury, who began the scheme, has now handed it over to a Trust, which lets the houses to suitable people, and proposes to utilise the profits, as they accrue, in the first place, to build more houses of a similar kind at Bourneville, and, ultimately, to buy land and to establish similar estates in other parts of the country.

As at Port Sunlight, the internal arrangements at Bourneville and their surroundings are almost ideal. Mr. George Cadbury, the founder of the Trust, has a strong belief in the value of gardening as a civilising influence, and he has arranged that each house on the estate shall have one-sixth of an acre of land. This land is carefully laid out and part of the garden is planted with fruit trees. Mr. Cadbury says that he has found town dwellers who moved to Bourneville took to gardening as a duck takes to water. A feature of the Bourneville Trust of interest to town dwellers is that it aims at purchasing land outside the towns where it is comparatively cheap and at restricting the density of population on area to a reasonable number, about 30 per acre.

There is still another way in which private effort may be made to help in the provision of houses, viz., through building and co-operative societies. Building societies and their methods are too well known to need more than a passing reference. They have in a large number of cases enabled the more prosperous among working men to build houses for themselves or to purchase houses. But they have also frequently enabled a man of little capital to become owner of a few houses, and this in many cases has bad results. Such an owner frequently finds himself unable to keep the property in good repair and a number of such owners may be a considerable hindrance to sanitary reform.

In a great many cases co-operative societies have established building society departments and have done the same work as the ordinary building society. In other cases the co-operative society has itself purchased land, laid it out, and erected houses which it has afterwards sold or rented to its members or others. Where the houses are sold, there is, unless some special pains are taken in laying out the estate and planning the houses little to differentiate this from an ordinary building society. But if such pains are taken and good houses are built on wide streets and with plenty of open space about them, and if the houses are only let to the members and others so that the society can always keep control over them, then a real contribution to the housing accommodation of the district will be made. The difficulty which many co-operative societies have in finding a field for the investment of their capital might well be overcome by the development of building estates on such lines. Several societies in England have carried out large schemes, notably the societies at Leeds and Woolwich. If the societies in and around Manchester were to acquire and develope estates of considerable size, giving special attention to the quality of the houses and their surroundings, a practical step towards the improvement of local conditions would have been taken.

(b) *Municipal Effort.* The existence almost everywhere of the housing problem and its persistence in spite of private efforts to deal with it have forced public bodies to attempt its solution. The powers given to Town Councils in Great Britain have been mentioned in a previous chapter. It will be remembered that they relate to (a) insanitary areas and houses and

(b) the provision of new houses. There is scarcely any town in which steps have not been taken to improve or to remove insanitary houses or areas. An owner is bound to put his property into a state of repair and make it sanitary on the instruction of the health authority, or, if he neglects to do this, the authority may do the work and charge it to the owner. Where an area is found to be insanitary a scheme for dealing with it has to be drawn up and an order obtained by the Town Council, which then, either by agreement or compulsorily, obtains possession of the property. The property may then be in whole or in part demolished. The improvement in the healthiness of the area when clearances of this kind have taken place is most marked and has been well exemplified both in have quoted (p. 30) the figures for Manchester and Salford. houses, at rents similar to those charged in the demolished houses and equally near the places of employment, available for those dishoused, they will crowd into dwellings already occupied near the cleared area, and thus again create insanitary houses and areas. In our towns, as we gather from the census returns, overcrowding exists to a considerable extent. We have quoted (p. 30) the figures for Manchester and Salford. We may infer from these either that there are not enough houses for the population or that there are not enough at rents within reach of those who overcrowd. From the Census figures, on the assumption that the average family consists of five persons, it would seem that there are more than enough houses for the existing population. It is also true that in some parts of the towns there are many unoccupied houses. We are, therefore, forced to the conclusion that there is a deficiency in house accommodation at rents within the reach of the working classes. To provide houses simply for those who are at present overcrowded would necessitate the building of thousands of houses. But, as we have endeavoured to show in our account of selected areas, many of the existing houses are unfit for human habitation. The two Town Councils are fully aware of this, and they are continually weeding out the worst houses. So long as there is a deficiency of house room, however, they cannot do much. It is of the first importance—indeed it is a

condition precedent to an adequate treatment of the problem—
that the Town Councils should set themselves to ascertain
accurately the extent of this deficiency.

Private enterprise, as represented by the ordinary builder
or by companies or societies like those described in the previous
section, has failed to supply the deficiency and there is no
evidence forthcoming that in the near future, under present
conditions, it will make it up. Year by year the natural
increase of the population makes matters worse. Apparently
the ordinary builder hesitates to sink capital in erecting houses
for those whose expenditure in rent can only be small. He
finds apparently the risks too great for the return he could get,
and if he builds workmen's dwellings, builds for the better
paid artisan.

Under these circumstances the community has to consider
what it can do to solve the problem. It may, through the Town
Council, acquire old property and make it habitable again, as
has been done by the borough of Camberwell; it may clear
insanitary areas and build houses on the cleared sites; or it
may acquire land, which may be within or outside the city
boundaries, and either get others to build on that land or
build there itself. The powers given to the Town Council by
law put it in a very strong position for carrying out any of
these schemes, since it can compel owners to sell land. With
the security of the rates, it can borrow money for building
at low rates of interest. On the other hand, the Town Council
is at a disadvantage in building, as the scheme and the detailed
plans have to be approved not only by the Council but by the
Local Government Board, and the inquiries necessitated by this
condition often lead to great delay in getting the work accomplished. The conditions of municipal building, too, are much
more severe than those of private enterprise, since the Local
Government Board rules are more stringent than local bye-laws.

If a Town Council decides to build it is faced with two
questions:—For whom? and Where? The Acts of Parliament
give power to provide houses for the working classes, but do
not define these classes. There is consequently a considerable
diversity in the dwellings erected by Town Councils. Some

Councils have aimed at building primarily for those whose earnings are low, and, it may be, irregular. In other cases, the needs of skilled artisans and craftsmen have been considered. The Acts, too, give the local authority a wide discretion as to the site of the building scheme, though this discretion may be limited by circumstances. The accommodation provided may be in the form of ordinary dwelling-houses or of special lodging-houses. Both Manchester and Salford have made part of their housing schemes, the provision of model lodging-houses for men, Manchester at Walton House, Ancoats, Salford at Bloom Street. The Manchester lodging-house has beds for 363 men, the Salford lodging-house for 285.

We may consider two cases which indicate the powers of the Town Council. In the one case, a Town Council may decide to deal with an insanitary or slum area under Part I. of the 1890 Act. In preparing a scheme, the Town Council is bound to consider the needs of the tenants to be displaced, and the Act states that the confirming authority (the Local Government Board in the case of provincial towns) may require provision to be made in the same area or near to it for the tenants dishoused.

In the second case, the Town Council, realising the need for providing good dwellings, may purchase land, under Part III. of the Act, either inside or outside the town boundaries and there carry out a housing scheme.

In most large towns, some action has been taken under Part I. of the Act in dealing with insanitary areas, and numerous examples can be found of good dwellings built by Town Councils on areas which were formerly covered by slums. In Manchester, work of this sort has been carried out by the Town Council in Ancoats, where the Oldham Road Dwellings and the cottages and tenements in neighbouring streets and the Pollard Street Dwellings replace property which was very insanitary. Similar work has been done in Salford, resulting in the Queen Street Artizans' Dwellings and the King Street Cottages. There is much to be said against rebuilding dwelling-houses on cleared insanitary areas. The worst slums, the oldest and most dilapidated property is usually near the

g

centre of the town. Year by year, the need of the business
community for office and warehouse accommodation and for
shops becomes greater, and land in the centre of the town, con-
venient for business purposes, naturally becomes more and more
valuable. It is consequently, as a rule, a very costly process
to house people on the areas which have been cleared. In
almost all cases the land is too dear to allow of the erection of
cottage property and there is not only the English dislike to
block dwellings to consider, but the recognised fact that these
dwellings are less satisfactory than well-built cottages, although
they may be infinitely better than the slum cottages which
preceded them. The cost of a housing scheme of this kind is
also increased by the compensation usually paid to the owners
of the property.

It is maintained in favour of schemes of this kind that
workers must live near their work, and it is therefore absolutely
necessary to provide houses on or near the spot for those dishoused. Of course, many workers like to live, and do live, near
their work, even when the surroundings must tend to lower their
value as workers, but, on the other hand, we have ample
evidence, not only from the results of our enquiries but from
the rapid growth of suburban residential districts, and from
the crowds who use the workmen's cars and trains to and from
town in the early morning, that a very large proportion of
workers do not live near their work. It is possible that market
porters and some others may have to live near their work, but,
even in those cases, the need requires proof. We have in
another place (p. 28) drawn attention to the overcrowding on
area which exists, and we have insisted on the need for more
space about dwellings. If buildings are erected on costly land,
it is obvious that less land can be given to each house than
where the land is cheaper, as it usually is on the outskirts of
a town.

The difference in the cost of land in the centre of the town
and in the suburbs is well illustrated by the history of Manchester schemes. The land in Ancoats, cleared and afterwards
built on, cost at Oldham Road £5 6s. 9d. per square yard, at
Pollard Street £1 14s. 10½d. per square yard, and in Hulme,

at Chester Street, the cost was £2 13s. 5d. per square yard. Two years ago the Town Council purchased about 238 acres at Blackley for £35,643 10s,, which is about 7½d. per square yard.

But a still greater difficulty in connection with housing schemes which involve clearance is that of finding accommodation for the people dishoused. Even if provision is made on the same site for those who occupied the houses which are demolished, there must be a considerable interval while building is going on when the people must find room elsewhere. Some will probably move away from the district, but, in nearly all cases, it is found that those dishoused crowd into neighbouring houses and thus make unwholesome conditions there.

It is, too, the common experience that a very small proportion of the tenants dishoused return to the area when the new houses, which must be more costly than the old ones, are erected.

We consider that the only satisfactory plan is for the Town Council to estimate carefully the deficiency in house accommodation existing and the additional deficiency likely to be created when unwholesome houses are closed. Steps should be taken to encourage the erection of good and wholesome houses, preferably in the less densely peopled parts of the town and in the country districts lying outside or just on the town boundary. Care should be taken in any scheme of the kind to provide houses of different types to encourage the movement to the outer districts of all classes of the community. When some progress has been made in this direction, the sanitary authority should be vigorous in demanding the closing of unwholesome dwellings, and, where areas are cleared, should endeavour to keep a considerable portion of the space unbuilt on as lungs for the crowded part of the town. In Salford, where a large number of areas have been cleared in recent years, we notice that many of these areas are advertised for sale as building sites. In our opinion it is highly desirable that the Borough Council should acquire some of these and retain them as open spaces.

In London, Glasgow, and Liverpool extensive schemes of clearance have been carried out and houses have been erected on the cleared sites. In London and Glasgow the new dwellings have in nearly every case been block dwellings. These schemes reduce the population on a given area and ensure well built and, subject to the drawbacks of block dwellings, wholesome surroundings.

In Liverpool an immense scheme is being carried out in one of the poorest quarters. For many years the Town Council has been at work on the district closing and clearing small areas and erecting dwellings of different types—in some cases blocks and in other cases cottages. In the most recently completed section of the work the new houses are built in three-storey blocks, each tenement having two or three rooms. The blocks have been carefully planned and arranged so as to give the houses the greatest possible amount of sunshine and air. Each tenement has a w.c. and an ashbin, and a central station supplies hot water to a tap in each house. The building is practically indestructible and should disease or vermin get in, a house can be " stoved " or washed down with a hose.

The policy in Liverpool has been and still is to try to house the poor and very poor in the crowded part of the town. Necessarily, therefore, houses which are both cheap and sanitary have to be provided. An experiment is now being made with the object of providing very cheap houses. A three-storey building is being erected at an estimated cost of about £100 per three room tenement. The material used is concrete formed of crushed clinker from the refuse destructors with Portland cement. The sides, floors and roofs of each room are moulded in one piece at the destructor depot, conveyed to the site of building and put in place. This experiment will be watched with great interest.

We have indicated above, however, our conviction that the most hopeful line of work is to take action under Part III. of the Housing of the Working Classes Act, and to provide dwellings without regard to any question of the clearance of insanitary areas, if it is shown that there is a need for more houses. As yet municipalities have not taken as much advantage of Part III. as might have been expected, but popular feeling seems now to have been aroused and it is to be hoped that progress may be rapid. The town of Richmond in Surrey has the honour of leading the way and the Richmond Scheme is now well-known. The Town Council there has built 119 cottages of six, five, and four rooms each. The external appearance of the cottages is pleasant and small gardens are provided. The rentals are low for houses of so many rooms, varying from 6s. to 7s. 6d. per week. Twelve cottage-flats were also erected, the ground floor houses being let at 4s. 6d. per week and the upper floor houses at 5s. 6d. per week. The scheme has been self-supporting.

London has several large schemes in progress at the present time, and in other parts of the country action is being taken.

The Manchester Town Council has acquired 238 acres at Blackley under Part III. The erection of houses is now proceeding, though there has been considerable delay in carrying through the scheme. The Manchester scheme, which provides for 203 cottages, has been carefully planned. Baths are to be provided in the majority of the houses, which will have three bedrooms. About one-third of the houses will have a large living room and small scullery, but no parlour, and the living rooms will be arranged to face the south, thus ensuring a maximum both of air and light in the room most used.

The houses will have small gardens, and allotments are being provided on the estate, which will be let to such tenants as require them. The scheme is intended to be self-supporting.

We are strongly of opinion that Town Councils should encourage building as much as possible and invite private builders and associations formed for the purpose to co-operate in the provision of wholesome dwellings for the working classes. The Act of 1900 gives the Town Council power, with the consent of the Local Government Board, to lease land acquired under Part III. The Act also states that societies, companies, and private individuals engaged in providing houses for the working classes may borrow money, not exceeding one moiety of the value of the estate or buildings to be mortgaged, and repayable within forty years, from the Public Works Loan Commissioners. It is to be noted that at the expiration of the lease the municipality would obtain complete possession of the buildings and that in the meantime as owner of the land it could insist on any conditions thought desirable as to the type and arrangement of buildings. Some provision, too, would have to be made for the efficient repairing of the dwellings, or doubtless the commonly-experienced difficulty that owners, near the end of a lease, will not spend money on repairs, would be encountered.

In Germany, the system of promoting the supply of wholesome dwellings for workpeople by the co-operation of building societies and others, who erect dwellings on land owned by the Town Council and largely aided by loans of capital at low rates of interest, has been widely adopted. (See Supplementary Volume.)

The Prussian Government, partly for the purpose of building dwellings for railway or other workmen employed by the State, partly for the purpose of lending to building societies or to Town Councils to be used by them directly or else lent by them to building societies, has in the recent past provided sums equivalent to £1,600,000, and purposes providing £600,000 more this year.

In Germany the law allows savings banks and the insurance institutions created in the new system of compulsory insurance of workpeople to use a considerable proportion of their vast funds in loans to building societies, and the power is largely used. One insurance institution has lent £545,000 to defray the cost of workmen's dwellings, charging from 3 per cent. to $3\frac{1}{2}$ per cent. interest. Some Town Councils promote the formation of building societies by taking some of their shares as well as by making them loans at low rates of interest. German towns possess much land and some Town Councils use part of the town land to aid building societies. They lease land to the societies at low rents for comparatively short terms of years—about 60 years—and also lend them nearly the whole of the cost of building. This can be done safely as at the end of the term of years the house becomes the property of the town to which the site already belongs. In some cases, too, part of the cost of street-making and sewering is remitted by Town Councils in favour of building societies. In the Rhine Province, building societies thus helped, provided 2,174 dwellings in the year 1901, which amounted to one-sixth part of the number of workmen's dwellings needed at that time.

In 1902, there were 113 building societies in the Rhine Province. Sixty German societies have erected 5,450 dwellings.

What strikes one on surveying the work done in English towns is that there is no well defined policy in dealing with housing. In dealing with water supply or tramways, some attempt is made to consider the needs of the whole town and a comprehensive scheme is drawn up even if the work has to be carried out in stages. But in housing the policy seems to be one of patching, and again, with possibly a few exceptions, we do not hear of a local authority making a comprehensive survey of the housing conditions and the housing needs of its district. Manchester and Salford both seem to fail in this respect. Yet the need of a clear policy is evident. Owing to lack of foresight, whole districts are being covered with houses and no provision is made for open spaces. On the fringe of the towns where other local authorities have control, and where building bye-laws are in some respects less restricting than in Manchester and Salford, much building has been going on in recent years. In these districts unwholesome and insanitary areas are being created, and the evil of bad housing conditions is being spread over a larger and larger area. It is highly desirable that the larger centres of population should have control over building conditions in their immediate outskirts. But even this power would be of little value unless a comprehensive policy had been adopted. In this respect German towns are far ahead of us. Nearly all large German towns have building plans. To the preparation of these plans, a large amount of thought and trouble is given and experts are frequently called in to advise.

The preparation of such a building plan involves several things which we have already urged or are about to urge. It demands, first, careful inspection to ascertain existing conditions and to enable reliable estimates to be made of the needs of the towns not only at the moment but in future years. In framing such an estimate, it is probable that the Town Councils would gain valuable assistance by appointing a special commission, comprising not only members of the Council, but other repre-

sentative citizens, which would examine witnesses and discuss
the subject from all points of view. Such a municipal
commission to deal with housing has been appointed by the
Town Council of Glasgow, at the instigation of Professor Smart.

The next stage would be to prepare for the whole district,
plans showing how it should be developed, indicating both the
houses and areas which ought, for convenience of traffic, for
health, or for general amenity, to be cleared, and also the lines
which should be followed by new roads and streets and the areas
which ought to be left unbuilt on. This may seem a big
scheme, but, as we have stated, it has been adopted in Germany.
It is our opinion that the policy of patching, *i.e.*, of dealing with
small areas or houses as attention is drawn to them, making
slight changes in bye-laws, or erecting small groups of houses,
while good so far as it goes, will never result in a healthy
Manchester or a healthy Salford. There should be a clear
understanding of what is being aimed at, even if the actual
work can only proceed by short stages.

In the preparation of building plans many large German
towns have now adopted the principle of zones. The more
distant a zone is from the central district of the town, the
smaller is the proportion of each site which may be covered
with building, and the smaller is the number of storeys allowed.
This arrangement has been seen to be so necessary, that the
kingdom of Saxony, by a most valuable Act of Parliament
passed in 1900, has made it compulsory for all towns in the
kingdom. (See Supplementary Volume.) It is recognised that in
the preparation of building plans for towns great attention
must be given to so arranging the direction of streets that all
dwellings may receive as much sunshine as possible. It is
also thought desirable to arrange that factories and other
" works " shall be confined to certain districts. Great efforts
are now being made to promote the erection of a large number
of small houses, especially of " one family houses " for working
people. The insistence on the need for leaving a large proportion of land uncovered in the outer parts of towns is due both
to the conviction that it is an arrangement necessary for the
health of the inhabitants of all parts of the town, and also to

the belief that, by thus making it impossible to house a large
number of persons on a given area of land, the price of land,
in districts where it is not already dear, is prevented from
rising as much as it would do otherwise.

As Mannheim is chiefly a manufacturing town and has
very carefully considered how it can increase its power to com-
pete successfully with other German and with foreign towns,
the arrangements adopted by its Town Council to guide the
growth of the town, if compared with the arrangements made
by our Town Council to guide the growth of Manchester, will
enable us to form an opinion as to whether the German or the
English system of municipal government is the more efficient.
The description of the building plan for Mannheim prepared
by Professor Baumeister, which is published in Nos. 69, 70,
and 71 of the *Centralblatt der Bauverwaltung*, shows that the
new part of the town will be provided with a remarkably complete system of railway lines of the ordinary width, leading
from goods stations in all directions, for goods traffic, which
will enable every manufactory to load goods on to trucks on its
own premises. Carriage, therefore, will be exceptionally cheap
in the town.

Yet the Town Council, who are thinking so much of
economical working, recognise that even their poorest citizens
are men and women, whose bodies and minds need wholesome
recreation and an abundant supply of fresh air, of light, and
of the influence of flowers and trees. The building plan, therefore, provides for the creation of avenue-streets of widths
varying from 24 to 43 yards, and Professor Baumeister adds :—
" Of course, care has been taken to provide open spaces,
decorative shrubberies, parks, and sites for public buildings."
The width of ordinary streets varies from $8\frac{1}{2}$ to $21\frac{2}{3}$ yards.

TRANSIT PROVISIONS.

A factor of increasing importance in the solution of
housing difficulties is the provision of improved means
of transit in our towns. All that has been said about
overcrowding on area and about the cost of land in the towns
emphasises the need for going with building schemes to where

cheap land is plentiful.   Such land is still to be found on the
fringe of our towns and beyond the town boundaries.   No great
movement of workers to the outskirts of the town can be
expected unless houses are plentiful and good, and there is
easy, quick and cheap communication with town.   The worker
need not live near his work if he can readily get to and from
it without unduly extending his working day.   Most town
dwellers, too, like to remain within easy reach of the amuse-
ments and interests of town and, unless this is possible, will
rather remain in town than suffer isolation.

Trains and tramways have for long made it possible for
many workers to live far from their work, but until a year ago
or less there was much room for improvement in our district.
The recent provision of electric tram services by the municipalities has, however, greatly extended the choice of dwelling
places for working men.

Should the tramway undertakings in Manchester and Salford succeed, as similar enterprises have done elsewhere, it
ought to be possible to imitate Glasgow and other towns and
greatly reduce the cost of travelling.   With fares at a halfpenny per mile and a penny for three miles, suburban residence
becomes possible for many workers.   The only other necessary
condition is that there should be an ample service of quick
cars.   This most towns are providing.   The scheme gradually
being developed by the Manchester Corporation of providing
through routes in every direction will do much to make the
use of the trams and of suburban residential districts popular.

The local train service opens many suitable residential districts to working men, but a considerable extension of the
service and reduction in fares is needed to make this as effective
as it might be.

It is very important that in the development of our tramway
system care should be taken to supply lines to thinly peopled
districts as well as those which have already considerable populations.   In this way the provision of houses may be
encouraged.   But it is also important that the departments of
our Town Councils should work in harmony, and that care
should be taken by those concerned with the provision of

dwellings to secure land for their erection before the tramways are extended in a new direction. As soon as the tramway is extended, often as soon as the scheme is formulated, the price of land near the lines goes up. This increase in value really belongs to the community which has made it, and it is fitting that so far as possible the community should reap the benefit of it. The provision of tramways or other means of transit will not by itself lessen the housing difficulty; cheap, good and comfortable houses are also wanted and these cannot be provided where land is costly. We urge, therefore, that the Housing Committees and the Tramway Committees should work hand in hand to provide opportunities for more wholesome conditions of life.

It is also absolutely necessary for the prevention of the growth of new overcrowded areas by the sides of new tram routes that careful building plans for the district to and through which new lines are to pass shall be prepared by the controlling authorities before the tram lines are constructed. The planning of town extensions has already been discussed. (See p. 89 *et seq.*)

BUILDING CONDITIONS.

New houses have to be erected in conformity with the local bye-laws which are based on the Model Bye-laws of the Local Government Board. Although such bye-laws have, as was intended, the effect of securing on the whole reasonably healthy conditions in the houses erected, yet, in some ways, they act injuriously on house building. In the first place, the tendency to build so as to provide the minimum requirements of the bye-laws largely accounts for the miles of houses of exactly the same pattern and appearance to be found in all our large towns. The lack of elasticity in the bye-laws prevents the builder from responding to the different demands of town and suburban conditions. The use of cheaper building material is also rendered difficult. Timber, concrete, and steel, all of which give opportunities for a much needed variety in the external appearance of houses besides being cheaper than the

ordinary brick or stone walls, can scarcely be used under the
existing regulations. In this connection reference should be
made to the Saxon Building Laws described in the Supplementary
Volume.

On the other hand, the bye-laws do little to regulate such
important matters as the area and cubic content of rooms. We
are glad to note that Manchester has recently (1902) obtained
sanction for a bye-law which provides that one room on the
ground floor of every new house shall have an area of at
least 144 square feet. But there is still need for a bye-law
regulating the cubic content of rooms intended to be used for
sleeping purposes.

Apart from the requirements of the bye-laws, there is need
for an improvement in the planning of houses. The interiors
of the houses in working class districts in Manchester and
Salford are not less monotonous than the exteriors. The
arrangement of space in a house has little or no relation to the
ordinary life of the family occupying the house. The living-
room or kitchen, frequently too small for the many functions
it has to serve in a working-class household, might, with advantage, be enlarged at the expense of the seldom-used front room
or parlour. The model houses at Bourneville and Port Sunlight are on the plan suggested, which has also been adopted
for some of the houses about to be erected at Blackley. Then
there is an obvious need for more houses with at least three
bedrooms, although houses with two may suffice for small
families. The desirability of every house being provided with
a bath is now generally admitted, but progress in this direction
is slow. This may in part be set down to the cost and the
difficulty of finding a suitable place to put a bath. In the
last few years several ingenious and comparatively cheap
schemes have been adopted. At Bourneville, in some cases a
bath has been sunk in the scullery floor and covered, when not
in use, by a trap door. In other places, a bath has been put
in the scullery and covered in so that it forms a sideboard or
table. An ingenious range and boiler, devised by Mr. Cornes,
of Leek, has made it possible for him to provide in some
cottages he has built at Leek a bath with hot and cold water

A MANCHESTER COTTAGE PLAN.

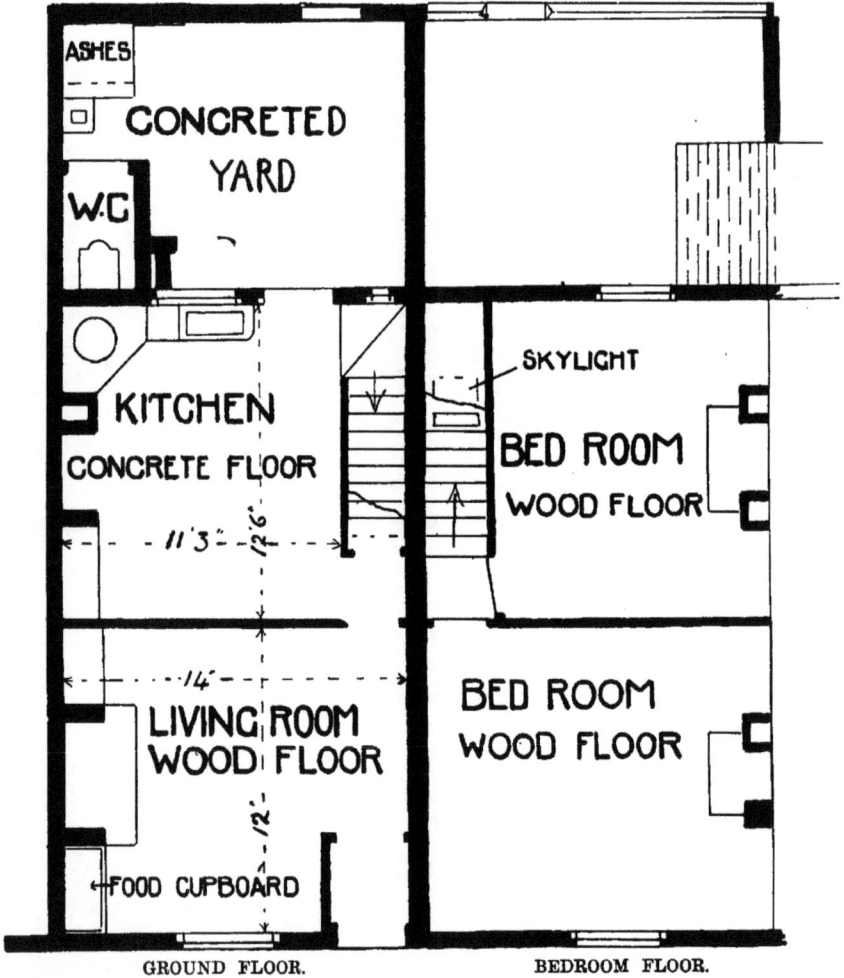

ASHES

CONCRETED YARD

W.C

KITCHEN
CONCRETE FLOOR

·11'3·   12'6·

·14'·

LIVING ROOM
WOOD FLOOR

12'

←FOOD CUPBOARD

GROUND FLOOR.

SKYLIGHT

BED ROOM
WOOD FLOOR

BED ROOM
WOOD FLOOR

BEDROOM FLOOR.

To face p. 95.

in the scullery at much less cost than with the ordinary arrangement.

It is not to be expected that the average builder will provide houses of the kind we suggest, especially as the public is apparently fairly contented with the houses at present built. But it would be well if Town Councils, in carrying out housing schemes, set a standard a little in advance of the popular demand by improving the plans and convenience of the houses. A comparison of the plans we give of a typical Manchester cottage and of a Port Sunlight cottage (see p. 78) will, we believe, be of interest.

CHAPTER VII.

LEGISLATIVE NEEDS.

Although municipalities have been given extensive powers for dealing with housing and generally for protecting health by the legislation of the last half century, experience has shown that further legislation is needed before it will be possible to solve the housing problem.

In various places in our report we have suggested courses which demand further legislation; at this point, we propose to summarise the legislative measures which seem to us to be needed now.

(1) There is primarily need for legislation in regard to land. Every inducement should be given to the municipality to acquire and hold land. In this connection the reforms needed are:—(a) The repeal of any clauses which compel the Town Councils to dispose of surplus land when improvement schemes have been carried out; (b) power to acquire land for future needs (at present land can only be purchased when it is actually required for a scheme about to be carried out); (c) power of compulsory purchase, at a fair market price, without compensation for compulsion (the present practice is to give 10 per cent. on the price for compulsory purchase); and (d) a simplification of the mechanism of " conveying " land.

It has been pointed out many times that dear land makes dear houses. Much cheap land, therefore, must be made available for house building if houses are not to be dear. This can be effected by the Town Councils purchasing land on the outskirts of the town while its market value is that of agricultural land or little more. It is the first duty of the municipality in dealing with the housing question to see that new houses are as wholesome and well-built as possible and that their surroundings are good, and for the provision of these conditions it is most important to have command of land.

It seems to us extremely desirable that, if Town Councils obtain power to buy land as they find opportunities, a separate

Committee, under the guidance of a competent salaried chairman, appointed for a long term of years, should be created to select, buy and manage the land acquired by the town; and that this Committee should have placed at its disposal a considerable sum, raised by loan, the interest on which should be defrayed by the income derived from the land bought for the town. This system has been very successfully adopted by the towns of Duesseldorf and Erfurt. (See Supplementary Volume.)

Another reform, desirable both because it would add to the wealth of the community and considerably increase the amount of land available for building, would much facilitate the compulsory purchase of land by Town Councils.

(2) The reform is the rating of unbuilt-upon land within the town boundaries. At present, rates are levied on the total ratable value of land and buildings, if the premises are occupied; but unbuilt-on land is not rated on its value as a site, but only on the sum which it produces annually. Many reformers suggest that the value of the land and the buildings should be separated and separate rates levied on them, and that, in the case of unbuilt-on land, a rate should be levied on its value as a site. We believe that a rate should be levied on the values of such sites as are not built on and are within the town areas, open spaces dedicated to the public use, gardens and allotments being excepted.

The pressure of population in our towns has largely increased the demand for houses. Land is needed on which new houses can be built. Such land as might be used for building purposes rapidly increases in value since the demand for land tends to outrun the supply. As unbuilt-on land is not charged with rates, some landowners prefer to hold their land, while its value rises, hoping later to obtain a high price for it. This holding of unbuilt-on land in towns is injurious to the community in two ways.

Firstly, as houses cannot be built on the land held, it increases the competition for other land which is open for building and sends its price up, and thus either ensures that houses built on adequately large sites are let at high rents, which cannot be paid by the working classes, or that houses

at low rents are built too much crowded together on the ground
and with a minimum of accommodation.

Secondly, the owner who holds up land does not make a
fair contribution to the local revenue. If his land is used
for grazing or other agricultural purposes, it is assessed
accordingly. Its value as agricultural land is low, and the
rates payable in that respect are at present reduced by half
under the Agricultural Rating Act. If the land is unoccupied,
no rates are paid at all. It is obviously unfair that land should
be rated at a nominal value, when its real value (*i.e.*, the price
for which it will sell as a building site) is being steadily raised
by the community. We, as we have already said, therefore
think that such land should be rated so that it may pay its fair
quota to the expenses of the town and in order that land may
be brought into the market. Another possible advantage is
that the assessed value for rating purposes might be taken as
the purchase price should the municipality think it desirable
to buy it, and the process of acquiring land might thus be
simplified.

In Germany, the rating of sites not yet built on has been
adopted by many towns. In the following passage, the results
of the system are briefly described :—" This system of rating,
which is so urgently needed in this country, was strongly
recommended, in 1899, to those German Town Councils which
had not already adopted it, by the Prussian Finance Minister.
It has been adopted by Crefeld, Breslau, Aachen, Duesseldorf,
Elberfeld, Charlottenburg, Kiel, Wiesbaden, and 62 other
German towns. Berlin, which has not yet adopted it, is said
to be about to do so. It is calculated that the introduction
of the system in Halle will have these results :—One owner
of building land worth £55,350, who now pays a rate of £1 14s.
a year, will have to pay £137 a year. Another speculator holds
land worth £72,300. He pays 13s. a year, and will have to
pay £179. In Dortmund, a speculator who used to pay 3s.
had his rate raised to £50 a year. When the new method of
rating was begun in Breslau, in 1900, speculators in land had
to pay an increase of rates of £15,250 a year. In Cologne,
under the old system, there were in one year 2,703 appeals

against 21,292 assessments. Under the new system of rating land at its selling value, there were only 174 appeals against 30,000 assessments."[1]

At a meeting held in Weissenfels on June 5th and 6th, 1903, Councillor Reimarus, of Magdeburg, where the rate is levied, thus summarised the advantages obtained by the introduction of this system of rating :—" (1) The rate on the selling value is free from the defects which come of the inflexibility of the old rate on land and the insufficient flexibility of the rate on buildings. (2) The new system of rating makes it possible to apportion the burden of rating more justly and more equally among the different classes of ratepayers than could be done before, and, in particular, it ensures a degree of rating of unbuilt-on land appropriate to the relation of that kind of property to other kinds, with the further result that the increased revenue thus gained can be used for lessening the rates on dwellings, and it abolishes the privilege hitherto granted to places of business, with the same results as have been mentioned. It establishes a right relation of the rating of the larger houses to that of houses of medium size and that of small houses, the last named having their rates considerably reduced."—*Soziale Praxis*, July 16, 1903.

(3) To encourage house building it must be made easy to obtain capital, and, unless the houses are to be let at rentals too high for the working classes to pay, capital must be obtainable at low rates of interest. It is highly desirable that Government should issue housing loans at lower rates of interest than are at present charged, and also that a considerable extension of the period of repayment should be permitted. The period of repayment at present varies from 30 to 60 years, and it is thought that an extension to 80 years for houses and to 100 for land might be made. It seems desirable also that savings banks should be encouraged to lend money to building societies which build under regulations approved by the Town Councils.

(4) It is very desirable that municipalities should have

---

[1] See "Ought Mayors, etc., to be paid salaries," by T. C. Horsfall, Manchester, 1903, p. 26. (Reprinted in Supplementary Volume, p. 31.)

h

power to insist on being notified of all proposed demolitions of house property, or of the conversion of house property into offices, etc., and that they should have power to insist on the provision of fresh accommodation before the demolition is proceeded with.

(5) Power should be given to a municipality to close the houses in a slum after accommodation has been found for the inhabitants and to remove the houses at the owner's expense. The justification of such a demand lies in the fact that a slum is a nuisance, often on a large scale, and is a menace to the physical and moral health of the whole community.

(6) The municipality should be compelled to insist in its building bye-laws on the provision of larger rooms in houses with, say, a minimum of 600 cubic feet of space per person.

(7) The Town Councils of large centres of population which tend to overflow their boundaries should be given power to supervise the building plans of the outside districts. Unless this is done it is quite possible for a series of slums to be created on the fringe of the town. Manchester-Salford, where there is a ring of authorities with different bye-laws, and with different policies in regard to housing surrounding the towns, is a case in point. In some of the outlying suburbs where the bye-laws of the local authority have not been sufficiently exacting, many houses have been built which simply spread some of the worst conditions of town life over a larger area. Power to incorporate such districts by an easier process than at present exists might, with advantage, be given to the larger towns.

CHAPTER VIII.

EDUCATIONAL AND RELIGIOUS INFLUENCES.

Thus far, our report has mainly dealt with what may be called the environmental side of the housing question. We have been discussing the external conditions required for healthy life, and have considered how far these are to be found in Manchester and Salford, and what steps ought to be taken to supply them in so far as they are wanting. But there is another side of the question to which we must devote some attention. To many social reformers this other side seems all important, and it must at least be admitted that nc effectual reform can be obtained by action simply from the outside. There is, for example, little use in providing good houses if the people who are to live in these houses do not know how to use them rightly, or if, by self-indulgence or from other causes, they nullify the benefit of good and wholesome surroundings. Nor will there be any marked tendency to supply good houses until there comes a real demand for such houses from people prepared to live full and decent lives if they can obtain wholesome dwellings.

It is fitting, therefore, that we should consider the agencies which are making for the improvement of the people themselves, and see how they help in the work of getting better houses and surroundings.

Among the chief means of effecting improvement of character and habits we put the influence of our schools. It should be an essential part of the work of every school to instil some knowledge of the conditions required for healthy life and a desire to live such a life. It is of the greatest importance, too, that due attention should be given to the physical development of the pupils attending school, to prevent, as far as possible, the bias to moral failing which is involved in physical weakness. We are glad to know that in our local schools this subject gets much attention. It is one of the most encouraging signs of the times that physical training in schools is often given in the open air, and we wish this could be carried further. It is of the greatest importance that people should get to feel at home in the open air and should resent being cooped up in unventilated rooms as are too many of the dwellers in all, but especially in the poorer, parts of our towns to-day. Interest in nature-study, with the corresponding developments of country rambles and window gardening, is to be looked on as another factor in helping towards a right appreciation of the conditions of healthy life. We wish, too, to urge the importance of giving the girls in the higher classes at school some instruction in the elements of house-keeping and in the conditions that are essential to the proper upbring-ing of children, the need for which has been strongly pressed by the Manchester and Salford Sanitary Association and by Dr. Niven. It is to be regretted that the opportunity for giving this instruction is so much limited by the early age at which children leave school. Much attention should be given to these subjects in continuation classes.

The need of cleanliness both of person and surroundings ought to be emphasised at school, as also the need for temper-ance. We are aware that attention is given to all these things in some schools in Manchester and Salford. We feel, however, that in every school in the district such training should be given, and now that a new start is being made in educational administration, the citizens should insist that health matters receive adequate attention. In passing we might suggest that the new Education Committees should at once see that all the rooms in all the schools are well ventilated, well lighted, and, in winter, well warmed.

An adequate staff of competent medical men should also be employed to attend to the physical and mental well-being of the children. It may be useful to mention that the town of Frankfurt-am-Main—a town of 289,000 inhabitants—has for some years employed 12 medical men to attend to the health of its scholars.

Much of the benefit derived from school training is lost during the period which intervenes between leaving school and the establishment of a separate home at marriage. This period of adolescence is most critical in the life of boy or girl. It is then that he or she begins to act on his or her own responsibility, since in most cases the adolescent is a contributor to the family income, if not entirely self-supporting. It is, therefore, of the utmost importance that there should be an ample supply of agencies continuing for young people the work of the school and strengthening and developing character along the right lines. Evening continuation schools, clubs, church and chapel organisations, and other institutions do most valuable work in this direction. We regret that there are apparently so few institutions of the kind for girls, and would urge that there is much need for an extension of work of the kinds done by many Sunday schools, boys' brigades, clubs, the organisations carried on by the Sisters of Charity, and other institutions.

We are informed by competent observers in different parts of Manchester and Salford that there is a regrettable growth in the prevalence of drinking and betting, and a decline in home life. Good surroundings may do much to counteract these tendencies, and we believe they would, but good surroundings will exist almost in vain unless there be some sturdiness of character to resist temptation and some feeling for the beauty and desirability of home life. The period of adolescence is the time when it is most necessary to stimulate these qualities.

We have so far been dealing with formative influences. As school and club become more conscious of their powers and duties, we may expect to trace their influence in the improved health and strenuousness of character of the community. But we have to consider also the adult of to-day. With the adult rests the responsibility of maintaining good conditions in the household and its immediate neighbourhood. We have in various places dwelt on the responsibility of the community as a whole for existing bad conditions, but the individual has duties towards the community and himself which are often not fulfilled. Many houses which we have examined would have been wholesome dwellings but for the carelessness and dirtiness of the tenants. An instance of carelessness is given in the illustration on this page from a photograph of the backs of some houses which have been put into good repair by the owner. The tenants, simply because they do not take the trouble to shut the ashpit doors, allow the back passage to become unwholesome. It is a common case to find a street strewn with refuse and garbage thrown there by the residents. No one is so ignorant as to be unaware that the street is not a suitable receptacle for refuse; such action can only be attributed to weakness of character and lack of public spirit.

The Ladies' Public Health Society does good work, through its visitors and the regular mothers' meetings, in stimulating individual effort towards the maintenance of good conditions in the home and street, and many churches and chapels serve the community in like manner. The Sanitary Association, the Ancoats Healthy Homes Society, and kindred bodies appealing to a wider public, also do much to help in getting and maintaining better conditions. More work of the kind is, however, urgently needed.

One of the most pressing needs of the time is a more vigorous and more widely spread spirit of citizenship. The most discouraging thing in relation to social reform is the apathy of the average citizen, and this holds true of the man who is well-to-do as much as of the man who is poor. Evidence of this apathy, if needed, is to be found in the existence of the conditions described in Chapters III. and IV.; in the high infantile death-rate, largely due to preventible causes, yearly reported by our Medical Officers of Health; in the slight interest shown in municipal elections and respecting the fitness for office of members of our Town Councils. There are good men on our Town Councils, but many members are merely the nominees of political parties and depend for their election not on their fitness for municipal work but on the strength of a political party in the ward. So long as such a system exists, so long will it be impossible to get the best men on our councils. We need, above all, men who are independent of party, whose primary aim is to put their experience and energy at the disposal of the community in efforts to improve conditions of life for the whole people.

In Salford. An example of the carelessness of tenants. Ashpits doors left open and refuse scattered in passage.

In Ardwick. A dirty yard. Ashplace without doors, and refuse strewn in yard.

Public opinion should make these delegates of the people use the power given them, and ensure that they do not fail in their duty to the community from regard for the interest of individuals or of a class. In this connection we feel it our duty to make an earnest appeal to all members of religious bodies to recognise the importance of good citizenship. We would especially appeal to the clergy of all denominations[1] to point out that it is the duty of every man to take his part in the work of the city, if not by serving it on the Council, at least by making careful and deliberate use of his vote for the return of the man best fitted to deal with the matters that are entrusted to the councils. Religion seems a mockery while men professing religious convictions make no effort to alter conditions of the kind described in this report.[2] Men need awakening to their duties toward their fellow-men, and need reminding that they have duties and responsibilities to the community. The common life of the town has given and keeps giving much to each individual citizen; he, on his part, should strive to give what service he may to the community. "If a man say, I love God and hateth his brother, he is a liar, for he that loveth not his brother whom he hath seen, how can he love God whom he hath not seen?"—1 *St. John* IV., 20.

---

[1] Citizen Sunday, which was recognised by about a hundred Churches in the Manchester district on the second Sunday of October, 1903, offers a special opportunity for emphasising the need for good citizenship.

[2] "How much of our terrible death-roll is due to the nature of the people's employment; how much to the state of their dwellings; how much to their home life—the personal habits of the occupants of our slums? These are some of the problems which confront us at the very threshold of our enquiry. Their solution will certainly tax our best energies—perhaps, indeed, it may at present be impossible—but we dare not shirk the attempt. The task which lies before us and our successors is nothing less than that of restoring to every infant in the Manchester Township the twelve years of life-expectation of which it has been defrauded by the evil surroundings of its birth." Dr. John Tatham in *Manchester Life Tables* (1893) p. 37.

APPENDIX A.

Investigator's Schedule.

CITIZENS' ASSOCIATION FOR THE IMPROVEMENT OF THE UNWHOLESOME
DWELLINGS AND SURROUNDINGS OF THE PEOPLE.

No. . ...*Street, Road, Place.*

1.—Description of House—
   Fronting Street or Court......... ..Back Buildings..............
   Old or New............................No. of Storeys ....
   Has House a good health record? ....
2.—Owner ....Address.................................
3.—Agent ....Address.................................
4.—Name of Tenant...
   Occupation ....
   Place of Employment ....
   Hours of Labour ....
   Places of Employment and Hours of Labour of other Wage-
      earning Members of the Household :

Give Wages of Tenant and Members of Household, if obtainable :

5.—Number of Persons in House—
   Males (Adult).................... Females (Adult)....................
   Children (under 14).....................................
   . Lodgers—Male......................... Female......................
6.—Amount of Rent per Week...
7.—Rooms.   (Number, size, position, etc.)

	(1) Size			(2)	(3) Position	(4) Lighting How many windows ?	(5) How is room occupied and used ?
	L'gth	B'dth	H'ght				
Living Room..							
Bedrooms I.							
II.							
III.							
IV.							
Kitchen							
Scullery							
Cellar							

Give dimensions of rooms in feet and inches, thus, 12ft. 6in. In
    describing position state on which floor room is situated, and
    whether it faces N. S. E. or W. Under 5 give particulars as
    to number of sleepers in room, and say whether (and what
    kind of) work is done there.
Is there any provision for keeping food fresh?..............................

8.—Condition of the House—
    Is it kept by Landlord in good repair?..............................
    Does the Teant keep the House clean?..............................
    Are any rooms damp?..............................
    Are any rooms dark? If so, why?..............................
    Does sufficient provision for ventilation exist in every room?......
    Do all windows open? ....
    Which rooms have fire-places?..............................
    Is there an oven? ....

9.—Sanitary Conveniences—
    What is the nature of convenience (W.C., Pail Closet, or Earth
        Closet)?..............................
    Where is it placed? ....
    What is its state of repair and cleanliness?..............................
    Is it used by others than Members of Household?..................

10.—Water—
    Has the House its own Water Tap?..............................
    Is there a Sink, and if so, where?..............................
    Is there a Copper or other provision for Washing Clothes?......

11.—Yard—
    Is there a Yard?..............................
    What is its size?..............................
    Is it Paved?..............................
    Well Drained?..............................
    Tidy? ....

12.—Nuisances—
    Are there offensive smells or disturbing noises, e.g., from
        Middens, neighbouring Factories or Shops, Public-houses,
        etc., or from work carried on in the House?

13.—Would occupation of present Tenant and his general circum-
    stances make it impossible for him to live in some other part
    of the town or suburbs?

14.—Notes.

Signature ....

APPENDIX B.

CITIZENS' ASSOCIATION FOR THE IMPROVEMENT OF THE UNWHOLESOME
DWELLINGS AND SURROUNDINGS OF THE PEOPLE.

MR. T. C. HORSFALL, M.A., J.P., *President.*

Bankers: WILLIAMS DEACON'S BANK LIMITED, St. Ann Street.

Vice-Presidents:

The Venerable Archdeacon WILSON, D.D.
Mr. W. J. CROSSLEY, J.P.
Mr. A. HOPKINSON, K.C., Vice-Chancellor of the Victoria
   University of Manchester.
The Rev. Dr. A. MACKENNAL.
The Rev. Dr. A. McLAREN.

Executive Committee:

Mr. T. C. HORSFALL, *Chairman and Treasurer,* Swanscoe Park, Macclesfield.

Councillor T. C. ABBOTT, Netherley, Bowdon
Mr. J. H. BROWN, Hale
Councillor D. BOYLE, 41, Carruthers Street
Rev. W. S. CAIGER, St. Mark's, Hulme
Prof. S. J. CHAPMAN, The Owens College
Mrs. CLAY, Carlton Lodge, Manley Road,
   Whalley Range
Rev. S. F. COLLIER, The Central Hall
Miss ALICE CROMPTON, The University
   Settlement, Ancoats
Rev. A. DALE, St. James-the-Less, Ancoats
Rev. D. DORRITY, St. Ann's, Manchester
Prof. C. H. HERFORD, The Owens College
Rev. T. T. JAMES, Lancashire College Settle-
   ment, Hulme

Rev. Dean O'KELLY, St. Anne's, Ancoats
Rev. S. NUGENT PERRY, St. Mark's, Holland
   Street
Rev. PRIESTLEY PRIME, 18, Hooley Range,
   Heaton Moor
Mrs. REDFORD, Wilholm, Chorlton-cum-Hardy
Very Rev. Canon RICHARDSON, Granby Row
Mr. J. SACKETT, The Central Hall
Rev. Dr. B. SALOMON, Norwood House, Hey-
   wood Street, Cheetham
Mr. FRED SCOTT, 83, Brazennose Street
Miss MARGARET SIMPSON, 20, Cannon
   Street
Councillor J. JOHNSTON, 14, Fennell Street

Secretary: Mr. T. R. MARR, 104, King Street, Manchester.

CONSTITUTION (Adopted 15th May, 1902).

Title. The name of the Association shall be "The Citizens' Association for the Improvement of the Unwholesome Dwellings and Surroundings of the People."

Objects. The Association exists for the promotion of Municipal and Housing Reform, and for the furtherance of an active spirit of Citizenship. It proposes to carry out these aims by any or all of the following means:—(a) By co-operation with the Town Council, and with other organizations concerned with the improvement of civic life; (b) by promoting the candidatures of suitable persons at municipal elections, and by taking such measures as will tend to secure a highly efficient and sympathetic Town Council; (c) by organizing public meetings and lectures for the discussion of civic problems; and (d) by such other means as the Association may sanction.

Membership. New Members must be proposed and seconded, and elected by the Executive Committee. Members pay a minimum subscription of two shillings and sixpence annually.

Officers. The Officers of the Association shall consist of a President, Vice-Presidents (not to exceed 10), an Hon. Treasurer and an Executive Committee, which (including the Vice-Presidents and other Officers) shall consist of not more than forty (40) members of the Association.

Secretary. The Executive Committee may, if it sees fit, appoint a paid Secretary.

Meetings. Meetings of the Executive Committee shall be held on the second Thursday in each month, at 3-30 p.m.

Ordinary Meetings of the Members of the Association shall be called at any time on the written request, addressed to the Secretary, of ten (10) Members of the Executive Committee, or thirty (30) ordinary Members of the Association.

An Annual Meeting, at which a Report and Balance Sheet shall be presented, and at which Officers shall be elected, shall be held during the month of February or thereabouts.

Financial Year. The financial year of the Association is reckoned from 1st January to 31st December, and Subscriptions are due and payable on 1st January of each year.

PROSPECTUS (issued in 1901).

" The Citizens' Committee* for the Improvement of the Unwholesome Dwellings and Surroundings of the People " is an association of persons desirous of effecting reforms, moral and material, in the condition of the poorer classes of dwellers in crowded and insanitary localities. Being founded in the City of Manchester, its efforts will be mainly directed to the local requirements of Manchester and Salford, but it does not seek to limit its field of influence when that influence can be usefully exerted over a wider area.

The aims of the Association are to arouse public attention to, and urge on the execution of, measures of utility, either by aiding and supplementing the efforts of existing organisations, or, when this cannot be done, by taking the initiative in respect of such measures. It is intended thus to supplement, not to displace, the work now carried on by various agencies, and so to utilise many means for the common end.

It is also intended to draw the attention of the City Council to cases where, in the opinion of the Committee, their present powers may be wisely used ; and, as occasion arises, to appeal to Parliament for extension or modification of such powers when desirable. Other means of extending the usefulness of the Committee may be used, none being excluded if they have the approval of the Executive Committee.

It is the object of the Committee to induce the Community to adopt all the measures needed to ensure that no buildings shall be

---

* The name was changed from " Committee " to "Association" when the constitution was adopted 15th May, 1902.

inhabited, in which, by reason of the condition of the buildings or of their surroundings, healthy life is impossible. These measures may be divided into two classes—(1) those needed to render the occupation of buildings, which are at present insanitary, compatible with health, or to ensure their removal; and (2) the measures which are needed to ensure that new buildings shall be rightly constructed and have wholesome surroundings.

As experience has shown that it is often impossible, without increasing the evils due to overcrowding, to close insanitary houses until new and wholesome dwellings have been provided for the inmates, the discovery and the adoption of the measures needed to provide an adequate supply of new wholesome dwellings and of the measures needed for the closing or improvement of insanitary houses are matters of equal urgency.

Hence the work of the Committee will include careful enquiry as to the causes which at present prevent the erection of a sufficient number of wholesome houses which must exist before any attempt can safely be made to deplete overcrowded areas. Right answers must be sought to such questions as the following:—

(a) Would not the erection of wholesome houses by public-spirited citizens be facilitated by the laying out by the Town Councils of Manchester and Salford of a number of wide streets, provided with a due supply of play-grounds and other open spaces; and the provision, by the same authorities, of tram lines or other means of quick transit at cheap rates?

(b) Do the Town Councils possess in sufficient measure the power to provide wide streets, open spaces, and means of quick transit?

(c) Do defects in our systems of land tenure, and of rating, or other hindrances, make it impossible or very difficult for the Town Councils to undertake such work?

(d) Does the administration of the licensing laws create obstacles to the erection of workmen's dwellings by persons of means and goodwill?

(e) If healthy dwellings at moderate rents, with good environment, and the means of rapid transit, were provided, would the proportion of the inhabitants of the central congested districts, who would be able and willing to remove to the new dwellings, be large enough to partly deplete the congested areas, and to enable the authorities to close insanitary dwellings without causing hardship to the occupants? An answer to this last question can be obtained only by careful house-to-house enquiry in selected test districts.

(f) What effect have slums on the physical, mental, and moral condition of those who live in them, and especially on the children who are born and bred there?

The Committee's enquiry respecting unwholesome dwellings will deal with the following points :—

What constitutes a slum? Is it the condition of the houses themselves, or the undue closeness to other buildings? To what extent is it the habits of the occupants which make a slum? What unhealthy dwellings are there in Manchester and Salford? To whom do they belong? Can they be put into such a condition as shall make healthy life possible in them? Are not large changes in and near unwholesome districts, such as the widening of streets, the provision of playgrounds or other open spaces containing vegetation, the provision of baths, and purification of the air, necessary to make healthy life possible? In what ways can the education in schools and the other training of the occupants be improved, so that they may co-operate with the rest of the community in putting an end to slums?

What rents are paid for such dwellings?

What return on the capital value do the owners of such property obtain? Has any considerable advance taken place in the rents of slum dwellings recently, and if so what are the chief causes of it? What unhealthy dwellings have recently been built, or are now being built, in and near Manchester and Salford?

In large German towns new streets are all very wide, many exceeding 28 yards in width, and many of them are planted with trees, and new building regulations provide that every part of every new building shall be adequately supplied with air and light. In Manchester and Salford new streets are only 12 yards wide, and large areas of the new parts of the town are left without vegetation. Is it not necessary for the physical and mental health of the inhabitants of all parts of the towns that fresh regulations respecting the width of new streets, and respecting the supply of air and light to buildings and the supply of vegetation shall be adopted here?

For the purpose of showing that towns can be so laid out and constructed as to allow healthy life to be lived in them, the Committee will obtain and disseminate exact information as to the system adopted in the building of such exemplary town districts as Port Sunlight and the districts created by the Messrs. Cadbury and by others, and also respecting the system adopted in certain Continental towns.

The Committee will also endeavour to acquire information towards the answering of these very important questions: Having regard to the immense importance and the great difficulty of having a wise and comprehensive policy systematically applied to the government of large towns, is it desirable to adopt here the system, which has been adopted in Germany and elsewhere, of appointing paid mayors, chosen for their efficiency, bound to give the whole of their time to the service of the town, and appointed for a long series of years? Ought not the incorporation of suburban districts needed to supply sites for dwellings and for public open spaces to be effected by a simple process by some local authority cognisant of the needs both of the towns and of the inhabitants of the adjoining districts? Are not much closer supervision of houses, and the provision of means to enable tenants to draw the attention of the authorities to defects in their houses or surroundings, necessary?

Should not the Medical Officers of Health, the officials who initiate prosecution for the production of smoke and noxious vapours, and the judicial authorities who try persons charged with such offences be appointed by the Government, so as to ensure that their action shall not be influenced by persons guilty of breaches of the law?

Would not an extension of the limit of composition for the rating of weekly-house property stimulate the building of dwellings of a satisfactory character? Is it not practicable to facilitate the maintenance of cleanliness, health, and comfort in workmen's dwellings by providing numerous wash-houses and baths in their midst, and by providing elementary schools, as is done in Germany and Switzerland, with shower-baths, and encouraging the scholars to use them regularly? Should not the Corporation be urged to establish, at rates such as those found practicable at Glasgow and Huddersfield, lodgings in houses from which tramps and persons known to be of immoral character and occupation shall be excluded? Cannot the evils of the public-house be largely diminished by the establishment of superior counter attractions in places where entertainments may be carried on and non-excisable refreshments and cheap suppers provided, such places not to close earlier than the public-houses?

For the collection of information the active exertion of our members will be indispensable; each must do his share, according to his abilities and opportunities in the amassing of facts from which we may proceed with confidence. Recourse must also be had to the Press, and to paid agents, for this end; but it is most desirable that our members should not, on that account, relax their efforts in our common endeavour.

All interested in this programme are cordially invited to become members of the Citizens' Association. The subscription is optional, subject to a minimum of half-a-crown yearly. Application for membership should be made to the Secretary, at 104, King Street, Manchester.

APPENDIX C.

A Brief List of Books on the Housing Question.

General.

"The Housing of the Working Classes," by E. Bowmaker. (London: Methuen, 1895. 2s. 6d.)

A simple introduction to the study of the Housing Problem.

"The Housing of the Working People," being the Eighth Special Report of the United States Government Commissioner of Labour. (Washington, 1895.)

This report can be seen in Public Libraries. It contains much information relating to housing laws and conditions on the Continent of Europe and in America.

"Public Health and Housing," by Dr. J. F. Sykes. (London: P. S. King, 1901. 5s.)

"Houses for the People" (No. 76); "The House Famine and How to Relieve It" (No. 101); "Cottage Plans and Common Sense" (No. 109) are useful tracts published by the Fabian Society, 276, Strand, London, W.C., price 1d. each. No. 101 contains a classified bibliography of the Housing Question, by Mr. Sidney Webb.

"The Housing Handbook," by W. Thompson. (National Housing Reform Council, 432, West Strand, London, 1903. 2s. 6d.)

The best and most recent study of housing. It contains accounts of the measures adopted by local authorities in dealing with the problem, and is written from the standpoint of a practical municipal administrator.

Housing and Poverty.

"Life and Labour of the People in London," by Charles Booth. (London: Macmillan.)

"Poverty: A Study of Town Life," by B. Seebohm Rowntree. (London: Macmillan, 1902.)

In these works careful studies are made of the conditions of town life, which are invaluable to serious students of the housing problem.

Legal.

"The Housing of the Working Classes Acts," by C. E. Allen. (London: Butterworth. 7s. 6d.)

Fully annotated texts of the Housing Acts.

"A Guide to the Housing Acts," by Arthur P. Poley. (London: Eyre and Spottiswoode, 1903. 3s. 6d.)

A handy up-to-date book of reference on Housing Legislation.

"Bye-Laws with respect to New Streets and Buildings."
Manchester. 6d.—to be obtained at City Treasurer's Office.)

"Bye-Laws with respect to New Streets and Buildings."
(Salford—to be obtained from Salford Town Hall.)

Statistics.

"Annual Report on the Health of the City of Manchester,"
by the Medical Officer of Health.

"Annual Report of the Medical Officer of Health for the County
Borough of Salford."

These annual reports contain much valuable information
as to the conditions existing in Manchester and Salford,
and ought to be better known. Special sections in each
report are devoted to the housing question.

"Manchester Life Tables," by Dr. John Tatham. New Edition.
(Manchester, 1893.)

*The Citizens' Association will gladly furnish information as to
other works dealing with housing and allied questions to those
interested.*

INDEX.

Lightning Source UK Ltd.
Milton Keynes UK
UKHW020826270223
417728UK00007B/681

9 781016 265362